Basic Gardening
A Handbook for Beginning Gardeners

Louise Carter

Lois & Janet
Welcome to our new
garden (& associated
house):
Daniel & Leslie

FULCRUM PUBLISHING
GOLDEN, COLORADO

To my daughters,
Charlotte, Sarah, Katherine and Lucy

Note: Some of the plants appearing in this book or appearing in nature may be poisonous. Any person, particularly a novice gardener, should exercise care in handling plants. The publisher and the author accept no responsibility for any damage or injury resulting from the use or ingestion of, or contact with any plant discussed in this book.

Library of Congress Cataloging-in-Publication Data

Carter, Louise.
    Basic gardening : a handbook for beginning gardeners / Louise Carter.
      p.   cm.
    Includes index.
    ISBN 1-55591-173-0
    1. Gardening—Handbooks, manuals, etc. 2. Gardening—United States—Handbooks, manuals, etc.   I. Title.
SB450.96.C37   1995
635—dc20   94-37915
                                CIP

Printed in the United States of America

0 9 8 7 6 5 4 3 2 1

Fulcrum Publishing
350 Indiana Street, Suite 350
Golden, Colorado 80401-5093

Table of Contents

Preface

Like me, my children have inherited a love and appreciation of gardens and gardening. In addition to all else, gardening is a gift to one's children, a means of communicating and learning between parent and child. I see it continue in my young grandchildren, who play under the willows, safari among the ornamental grasses and bring me bouquets from the fields.

Introduction

There are many meanings of the word *garden*: the Garden of Eden, that special place within a larger property where you grow flowers, the humble plot where you grow vegetables in the backyard. Here the word *garden* is interpreted to mean in the broadest sense the place where you cultivate plants. *Gardening* is the relationship between you, the gardener, and the plants that you grow. Many gardeners are thrilled to sow a few seeds in the ground and watch them sprout and grow, producing flowers or food. Others are more ambitious and wish to organize a wider corner of the world according to their personal vision.

For all, there are basic ways and means to make the experience of gardening and growing plants a happy and successful one.

Regardless of size, shape or geographical location, all gardens have in common certain basic requirements that must be met for plants to grow well. Variables in gardening mean there are no absolute answers to many questions. Some plants will not grow no matter how carefully you select, plant and maintain them, but there are many plants to choose from and most, given half a chance, will thrive. If you are an inexperienced gardener, start with annuals, which give an immediate effect and do not require a major investment. If you are not satisfied with your choices, you can experiment with a different selection next year. Or, try a mixture of plants that grow well together under the same soil and moisture conditions, such as a small mixed border with a flowering tree or shrubs in the background, a few easy perennials, some annuals for immediate color and bulbs to be added in the fall to produce flowers the following spring. As you gain an understanding of the growing conditions on your property and familiarize yourself with a group of plants that do well for you, it will be time to think on a grander scale.

All gardeners, inexperienced and experienced, must start by learning something about the site where they garden, its growing conditions, the choice of plants suitable to plant under those conditions and how to maintain them once they are planted. Your choice of plants will be limited by your climate, soil type and the amount of sun or shade and moisture readily available. The layout of your garden will be based on its size and topography and your personal preferences in plant material, foliage textures and flower colors.

This is not a book about designing a garden as such, except in the most basic ways, as design is determined by site conditions, by plant selection and their cultivation, and by maintenance considerations. This book will answer questions about gardening and growing plants. Some of the chapters may not pertain to your current gardening interests; others may seem too complicated if you have never planted anything before. Read the chapter headings for a useful overview and for future reference as you become more accomplished and your thumb grows greener.

Gardening is not difficult whether you start with a plant in your hand or with an empty space needing to be filled in the garden. Many plants will grow happily with very little attention. Many more will grow and flourish if you choose them properly and if you follow simple planting and maintenance guidelines. You can have a garden, large or small, in the ground around your patio or house or in containers on a rooftop or balcony. This book will get you off to a sound start. The important thing is to begin.

Your garden will become a setting in which you enjoy working and relaxing. It will be manageable and healthy, a place where you will find something of interest in color and form throughout the twelve months of the year. It can be a garden of many colors or just a few colors, an oasis with fragrant blossoms, with fruits and vegetables to harvest for the table, where even in winter you can find colorful bark and interesting silhouettes against the winter sky. The choice is up to you. As the year comes round and before the air warms, if you plan ahead, you will have a view from your window of the first spring bulb.

Chapter 1

Getting Started

Evaluating the Site

Whether you are starting within a framework of established trees or from scratch in an empty lot, whether working impulsively, or with a plan, you must consider the environmental characteristics or the growing conditions in your garden, choose appropriate plants for those conditions and plant them correctly. Ultimately, success depends on working with your soil type and water table (the amount of water present in your soil).

Use the following outline as a guide in evaluating your site and as a basis for preparing a simple workable plan. Conditions vary among different regions, even within your garden, particularly if you are dealing with a large space.

Note the following environmental factors as they will limit or modify the choice of plants that you can grow successfully in your garden. Many of the following contrasting situations may occur to some degree somewhere in your garden.

Light. Is the site sunny or shady? Is there sun all day or only half a day? Are some areas in partial or dense shade all day?

> Full sun: 8 hours to a full day of direct sunlight.
> Partial sun: 2 to 3 hours a day when no direct sunlight shines on the plant, or when a pattern of shade from young or very open trees lightly shades the plant. (Afternoon sun is stronger than morning sun.)
> Partial shade: 4 to 5 hours when no direct sun falls on the plant, or dappled light all day.
> Full shade: shade all day or reflected, indirect light, perhaps from the wall of an adjacent building.

Dense shade: no direct sunlight all day and little reflected light (north side of a building, or beneath heavy evergreens).

Some modifications can be made. Large trees can be limbed up or thinned out to allow more light to reach the plants beneath. Conversely, shade trees, large shrubs or trellises and pergolas with vines can be added to provide more shade.

Exposure. Is the site exposed or sheltered from prevailing winds and burning sun?

The chilling and drying effects of wind can severely damage plants. Lack of shade from summer or winter sun can cause burning and scalding of bark and foliage. Only a small number of plants can survive under those conditions. Heat reflected off large paved areas or building walls can burn plants, but it can also provide warmth for early spring flowers. Buildings and thickly planted areas may offer protection from wind and sun, creating microclimates (small areas within the larger area that enjoy climates generally hotter or colder than the norm for your zone), in which you can grow either more tender plants or more hardy plants, depending on conditions.

You can plant trees and shrubs, or build fences, to provide windbreaks. Evergreen trees and shrubs will provide shelter all year. Deciduous trees will shade and cool an area in the summer while permitting the sun to warm it in winter.

Soil structure. Is the soil loamy, sandy or mostly clay? Does the soil dry out or stay moist?

Good garden soil (loam) should have a suitable texture, or friability, to allow easy digging and the slow steady passage of water and nutrients through it to the root zone of plants. When you pick up a handful of good soil, it should form a ball, and the ball should fall apart easily when dropped. Sandy soil will not stick together. It drains well but dries out in summer and does not hold nutrients. Clay soil sticks together in clods and, while generally rich in nutrients, retains water, which can cause root rot, especially in winter.

Most land in the United States is composed of clay-loam soils. Soils in some southwestern regions are largely sand with very little silt and organic matter. In eastern regions, rocky, clay soils are the norm. Trying to change the nature of the soil of a large planting area is an uphill struggle, although modifications can be made in single planting beds.

Soil chemistry/soil pH. Is the soil acidic, neutral or alkaline? The pH scale, which ranges from 0 to 14, measures the acidity or alkalinity of soil. Zero indicates the maximum acidity, and 14 indicates the maximum alkalinity level. A reading of 7 is neutral. To enable your plants to absorb the nutrients they need for growth, the soil must have the appropriate pH balance. Most plants, including most perennials, annuals, garden vegetables and lawn grasses, prefer a neutral to slightly acidic soil. The major exceptions are ericaceous and other acid-loving plants: azaleas, blueberries, camellias, deciduous magnolias, heather, hollies, hydrangeas, leucothoe, mountain laurel, pieris, rhododendron, sourgum and sourwood, which prefer a pH of 4.5 to 5.5. Among plants that prefer alkaline soil, pH 6.5 to 7, are European ash, lilac, clematis and perennials such as bearded iris, bergenia, delphinium hybrids, dianthus, peonies and sage. Acid soils are most common in areas of high rainfall, in the East and Pacific Northwest. In the arid West, most soils are alkaline soils with pH levels between 7 and 8.

Soil structure and pH balance can be modified by the additions of organic and inorganic materials. For further discussion of soils, see Chapter 3.

Temperature zone. From the USDA Zone Map on page 125, find out the temperature zone in which your garden is located. This will enable you to choose plants hardy enough to withstand local winter weather conditions. It will also tell you the length of your growing season (number of frost-free days).

Developing a Plan

For a more comprehensive study of your site, take an inventory of specific landscape features or outstanding topographical features of the terrain: slopes, flat areas, rock ledges. Note views in or out of the property that you want to frame or hide as well as views from the house into the garden. Record plants that you may wish to save or remove.

This additional information will assist you with future planting plans, in locating family recreation and entertaining areas, organizing traffic patterns and gaining easy access to service and storage areas.

It is never too soon to consider future maintenance requirements and the amount of time you want to devote to the upkeep of your garden. A few suggestions follow:

Choose plants suited to local conditions. Buy the largest plants you can afford for a mature look. Combine plants with similar cultural requirements together in the same bed.

Keep labor-intensive lawn areas, perennial and annual plantings to a minimum. Plant unused lawn areas with trees and flowering shrubs. Use ground-cover plants in areas difficult to maintain.

Plan the size and shape of lawn areas and planting beds for ease of mowing. As lawn mowers and weedeaters are the major killers of young trees and shrubs, locate them in planting beds, or surround them with a circle of mulch.

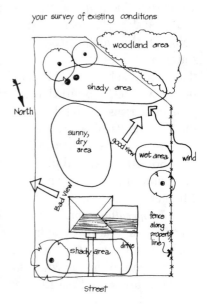

your survey of existing conditions

Planting beds wider than 4 feet are difficult to reach across for maintenance. Wide beds should have an access path at the back.

For gardeners who are interested in growing vegetables, a 450-square-foot vegetable garden is a manageable size. It needs full sun with a convenient nearby water supply.

Install an irrigation system. Plan to direct runoff rainwater toward thirsty plants, or collect it in a pond for future use.

Locate compost piles and storage areas for easy access but in unobtrusive places.

Plan a walkway—mulch, stepping stones, brick or other paving—around your house and to frequently visited spots in your garden so you can keep your feet dry in wet weather and prevent wear and tear of the lawn or ground covers.

When you have completed your study, draw a simple map (to scale on graph paper) identifying the different ecological areas in your garden: sunny and shady positions, dry, damp and exposed spots, po-

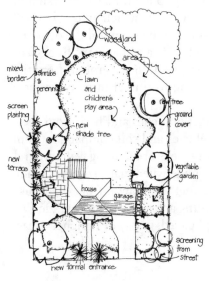

solution plan

woodland area

mixed border

shrubs & perennials

screen planting

lawn and childrens play area

new shade tree

new tree

ground cover

new terrace

vegetable garden

house

garage

new formal entrance

screening from street

tential problem areas where some adjustments must be made—erosion, water runoff, windy areas, etc. Locate any other permanent or planned features. Photograph or videotape your garden as a record for future reference and to help in the design process.

This thorough examination of your garden may seem daunting as you begin, but it will familiarize you with all aspects of your property and its growing conditions. Whether you want only the simplest planting space, or if you intend to embark on a long-term project, you now have the necessary site information with which to start. You will be able to choose planting areas correctly and site plants that can thrive under existing conditions.

Protecting Existing Plants

Plants die from major changes in their environment, so if your garden plan includes new construction and site alterations that change the exposure, grading and drainage conditions for existing plants, you should take steps to protect them.

Rapid clear-cutting of a wooded site leaves the remaining plants vulnerable to environmental change, to drier soil, to root damage and wind. As much as one third of plants remaining on such a site may die during the following few years from this sudden exposure. Try to save trees in groves instead of singly.

Grade changes alter drainage patterns and the moisture content of the soil. Even adding wooden decks and extending paving reduces the extent of areas formerly able to absorb rainfall; this affects plants nearby. Changing the grade over tree roots or cutting major roots during excavation can kill or cause severe branch dieback and decline of large specimens. Rope off areas surrounding trees and shrubs to prevent soil compaction from heavy equipment. These areas should be large enough to encompass the feeder roots which extend beyond the drip line of the plant, as much as twice the extent of the drip line or farther on mature trees. The drip line is an imaginary line, basically circular, indicating where raindrops fall to the ground from the outermost branches. It is less damaging to tunnel directly under a tree than to trench heavily nearby.

Roping off areas will also protect branches and bark from accidental damage from construction vehicles and soil compaction from stockpiled building supplies. Build tree wells or retaining walls around major trees to maintain the original grade when making severe grade changes. Plan surface drainage to funnel water away from the house and to fan out gradually toward planting areas. A 2 percent grade (1/4-inch fall per foot) will move water off paved, grassy or mulched areas.

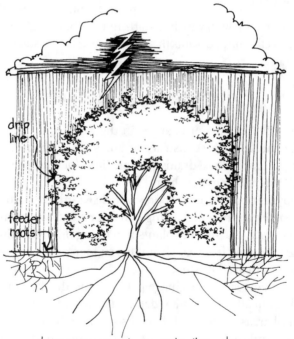

drip line

feeder roots

tree canopies act as umbrellas during rain storms

Choosing and Siting New Plants

Before you make your final decisions when choosing plants for the garden, reconsider the basics: plant hardiness, soil, light and moisture requirements, eventual size, seasonal interest and cultural and aesthetic compatibility with other plants in the same grouping.

Plants die from poor planting: being set too high or too deep, in a hole that is too small, thwarted by soil that is too heavy, rocky or shallow. They also die from too much moisture in the soil or too little, or from lack of water before they become established. Plants that are poorly adapted to a site and its growing conditions will be under stress and are more susceptible to insects and disease.

Plants die from improper siting, from putting a plant in the wrong place. Changes in the interaction between sun, wind and temperature throughout the year are vital to the well-being of any plant. Winter winds and sun desiccate plants, especially needle and broadleaf evergreens. Late frosts in low-lying dips may nip the flower buds on tender ornamental trees and shrubs which may then fail to bloom or fruit. Persistent summer sun and drought weaken woodland plants.

Anything you can learn about a plant's native habitat, or the conditions to which it is adapted, will make you a better gardener, enabling you to choose plants wisely, site them properly and install them correctly.

Chapter 2

Plant Groups and
Their Roles in the Garden

Gardens are composed of plants, different kinds of plants creating different layers within the garden and fulfilling different roles within the scheme. Trees are the canopy or upper layer, shrubs the background or intermediate layer. Ground-cover plants form the layer that joins the background shrubs with the ground level, which may be grass or paving.

Plants are divided into groups according to size and growth habits: trees, shrubs, vines, perennials, annuals, bulbs, herbs and vegetables. They can also be defined by the roles they play in design: major trees for shade, ornamental trees and shrubs for seasonal interest, deciduous or evergreen hedging plants for privacy and to define spaces, ground-cover plants to link and accent horizontal spaces, vines for vertical interest, and so forth.

Deciduous trees and shrubs shed all their leaves in autumn or in a dry season. A broadleaf evergreen (i.e., aucuba, camellia, holly) is an evergreen plant with wide leaves as opposed to a needle or thin-leaved evergreen (i.e., pine, spruce, fir). Evergreens shed their leaves slowly throughout the year, remaining for the most part green, although seasonal heavy needle drop is characteristic of pines. Some plants that are evergreen in warm

layering :
trees, shrubs and ground cover

climates lose many or all of their leaves in colder areas (i.e., abelia, bayberry, privet).

If you have a design or maintenance problem in your garden, you may be able to resolve it by choosing the right type of plant from one of these groups. In new gardens the problems are often a lack of shade and privacy, confusing spaces or traffic patterns, unattractive or ill-defined views or empty spaces. Older gardens become overgrown; the plants grow out of scale; foundation plantings become crowded, obscuring the doors and windows. Lawns are shaded out. Trees and shrubs have been neglected, their variety reduced by age or exposure or overtaken by "volunteer" weedy plants. The soil may be compacted and worn out. Areas of erosion may have developed. Then you must ask, "What do I remove or replace?" By understanding how plants can be used in the garden and how they grow, as well as how to nurture them, you can begin to sort out some of these problems as you develop or redefine your garden.

To further your general knowledge of gardening, study books and magazines on plants and horticulture as well as mail-order plant and seed catalogs. Many newspapers have weekly gardening columns. Visit your local arboretums, parks and public and private gardens to see what plants flourish in your area. Note pleasing combinations of plants, of foliage textures and color, plant structure and growth habits in public and private gardens you have seen.

Bear in mind the growing requirements of any plant you are considering. Questions to ask at the garden center or nursery are: Does it prefer sunny or shady light conditions? rich or poor, dry or moist soil? acid, neutral or alkaline pH levels? Is the plant evergreen or deciduous, perennial or annual? How high and how wide will it grow? Is it prone to serious insect and disease problems? If you are ordering from a distant nursery, check to be sure the plant is winter- and summer-hardy in your area (see the Zone Map on page 125). As common or local names vary across the country, note both the plant's common and botanical names so you can identify it correctly in case you want to find more, or avoid ever mistakenly acquiring it again.

Before finalizing your choice, here are some practical matters to consider: If you are choosing a shade tree or ornamental tree, will it stay in scale with your house and property, or grow too large for the garden, perhaps shade out the lawn? Will it overhang the house, become entangled in overhead wires? Will you be able to walk and mow comfortably under it? Will it drop messy fruit or seedpods on the patio? Will the leaves clog swimming-pool equipment? Do you need shelter from winter sun and wind? Would evergreen trees and shrubs rather than deciduous ones provide better shelter and screening throughout the year? Will your plant choices demand heavy pruning to be kept in bounds, or require too much water? Do you need a wider range of plants for greater seasonal interest? Would a group of ground-cover plants reduce erosion and maintenance on the hillside which is difficult to mow? Can you cut back on maintenance by reducing the lawn area and adding a mixed tree and shrub border?

Some plants are fussy, but most are tolerant of a wide range of conditions. To a certain degree, site conditions can be altered to accommodate certain plants, but it is generally wiser to work within the limitations given you. Choose disease-resistant and time-tested varieties or those recommended by your garden center, arboretum, horticultural society or local cooperative extension service. Try native plants for easy maintenance and to reduce watering and spraying for insects and disease. Choose plants whose ultimate size and shape are suitable for the planting site to avoid the necessity of future heavy pruning or transplanting. To reduce maintenance, group plants with similar soil and watering requirements in the same bed. All plants have minimum spacing requirements for healthy development of roots and tops. Good air circulation discourages plant diseases. Do not overcrowd plants.

Trees

Trees are the longest-lived plants in the landscape and in your garden, the most permanent element. In silhouette, in leaf form and in fragrance, they provide a sense of place—from the birch and sugar maples of New England, to the handsome firs of the Northwest, the moss-covered oaks and pines of the South across to Texas, the river bottom cottonwoods of the Plains and the shimmering aspen of the Rocky Mountains. It would be difficult to imagine southern California without eucalyptus trees although they are not native to the area. Even the sound of wind passing through trees differs, depending on the texture of the foliage.

Trees form the upper story, the canopy, of your garden. They suggest the character, sense of scale and the privacy of your garden. They are the link between your property and the neighborhood. To create a greater sense of space, use trees native to or common in your neighborhood to blur the transition between properties and, in rural areas, the abrupt change between cultivated and natural landscapes. There are deciduous, needle and broadleaf evergreen trees. There are trees for deep shade and for light and dappled shadows. Trees vary in density from heavy-headed, thick-leaved linden to airy acacia, jacaranda and moraine locust. They offer different moods. Evergreen oak and beech are stately; willows weep gracefully, adding motion to the garden. Palms are fanciful, decorative, rustling. Trees highlight different seasons. Cherries and crabapples bloom in spring. Sophoras bloom in summer. Maples, ash and sassafras add brilliant colors to fall gardens. After leaf fall, aspen, birch, Chinese elm, yellowwood, stewartia and many Japanese maples show interesting bark.

Trees vary in leaf texture and color from finely cut Japanese maples to coarse sycamore and compound-leaved goldenrain. Hollies and evergreen magnolias are noted for thick, shiny, deep green leaves. Russian olive and linden have gray-green foliage, plum and some crabapples have red foliage; 'Sunburst' moraine locust has yellow-green foliage.

Small ornamental trees—dogwoods, crabapples, cherries, hawthorns, Japanese magnolia—are chosen for a combination of qualities, for bloom, fruit, bark and fall color.

Needle and broadleaf evergreen trees provide year-round privacy as well as background for deciduous trees and shrubs. They can be used as specimen trees to stand alone and are particularly effective in winter. Needle evergreens vary in size from dwarf alpines to giant redwoods, in needle color from silver-blue spruce to yellow false cypress, in silhouette from columnar arborvitae to spreading atlas cedars.

Trees aid in climate control by protecting our houses from chilling winds. They provide shade for us in summer, cooling our houses, patios and terraces. They shelter the plants in our gardens from burning sun, including the grass on our lawns. They block out bad views, frame pleasing ones. They provide nesting places for birds and squirrels.

Trees generally have a single trunk or stem but can be multistemmed. At maturity they range in size from 25 to 200 feet or more. Trees may have branches to the ground or be "limbed up" by pruning as street and shade trees are. The distinction between trees and shrubs becomes blurred with plants in the 15- to 25-foot range. Plants such as crape myrtle, flowering magnolias and small maples may be listed in either category.

Trees are more expensive to buy and plant and require more time to establish after transplanting than shrubs, but they make an immediate impact from the moment they are installed. Although they need attention less frequently than smaller plants, due to their eventual size, they may require professional care for pruning, deep-root fertilizing and spraying.

Shrubs

Shrubs are the backbone of most gardens, providing texture, pattern, form and color. They create the understory level, or the background, filling in the space between trees and ground. Low-spreading forms function as ground-cover plants. Shrubs can be used individually or in groups to contour and outline the garden, defining and enclosing the property and marking divisions within it. They make loose informal or clipped formal hedges. They provide backgrounds for flower beds, define paths and borders.

Shrubs differ from trees in being more frequently multistemmed although they are sometimes pruned to a single stem, a form called a "standard." There are shrubs for sunny and shady locations, moist and damp sites. Like trees, shrubs are either deciduous or evergreen. Deciduous spring- and summer-flowering shrubs offer seasonal change. Broadleaf or needle evergreen shrubs provide permanent coverage and protection throughout the year.

Choose shrubs for their overall form, leaf texture and color rather than for their bloom, which may be of short duration. Choose them for multiseasonal interest: sometimes-fragrant blossoms (ceanothus, lilac, gardenia, some azaleas), colorful fruit (callicarpa, nandina, viburnum spp.), changing fall foliage (abelia, aronia, *Euonymus alata*), interesting bark (crape myrtle, kerria, parrotia) and winter silhouettes. Shrubs range in height from low compact spreaders of 6 inches to loose, open spreading specimens of 25 feet. They can be limbed up and thinned to reveal bark and stem formations.

Shrubs naturally grow in the following forms:

- pyramidal (most conifers, many holly species): use as free-standing or accent plants.
- columnar (upright yew, Japanese holly, arborvitae, pittisborum, buckthorn): use as accent plants in narrow places or as hedges.
- prostrate, spreading or weeping (rambling rose, cotoneaster, spreading yew, winter jasmine, juniper, lowboy pyracantha): these horizontally growing shrubs make excellent ground-cover plants on difficult slopes or banks, and accent plants as they cascade over a wall or rock.
- compact, round-headed (barberry, boxwood, juniper, Chinese and Japanese holly, cherry or Grecian laurel): use as hedges, screening and filler plants to add a civilized formal look.
- mounding, fountainlike, cascading forms (many deciduous, spring- and summer-flowering shrubs (spirea, forsythia, rose, weigelia, buddleia): use to add a casual natural look to an old-fashioned border, a mixed border or informally in clumps on a hillside.
- upright, multistemmed (lilac, crape myrtle, privet, althea, melalucca viburnum): use these large shrubs, often trained to look like miniature trees, for emphasis in formal plantings, as specimens in beds of ground covers or in containers.

Vines

Vines or climbers fill a special niche in the gardening scheme. Demanding little soil surface, they occupy vertical spaces, growing upward into the light. They add greenery and color to walls and fences, pergolas and trellises. They attach themselves with tendrils, short stems that wind around other plants or wires for support, or rootlets that cling to walls of stone and brick. There are annual (morning glory, moonflower, scarlet runner bean), perennial (clematis, climbing hydrangea), evergreen (ivy, ficus, euonymus) and deciduous vines (wisteria, Boston ivy, Virginia creeper).

Many vines become bare at the bottom as they develop, and some may need their roots protected from the heat of the sun. Underplant them with low-growing shrubs or flowering ground covers, choosing ones that blossom at different times than the vines to prolong interest.

Annuals, Biennials and Perennials

Annuals, biennials and perennials are part of the ground level of the garden. They provide an element of seasonal change. They can be chosen to blossom during different months of the year. Many perennials are worth including in the planting scheme for their interesting foliage alone. Many are useful in containers.

Annual plants complete their life cycle within one year. During that year they start as seed, grow, flower and produce fresh seed to begin the cycle over again.

Annuals are used more for blossom than foliage, for temporary brilliant or pastel seasonal effects, by themselves in formal or informal beds or as off-season fillers. Use them in containers from window boxes to hanging baskets and in new beds to fill gaps until the permanent plantings fill in.

Biennials complete their life cycle within two years. Starting from seed the first year, they grow and die down during the dormant season, reappear again the second year, flower and go to seed. They can be used in design in the same manner as perennials but will have to be replaced.

Perennials are herbaceous, or nonwoody, plants that die down to the ground in winter, sometimes leave a rosette of leaves, or sometimes disappear completely. Their roots continue living underground during the dormant season, and the plants return in the spring to grow and flower again. In warm climates, some perennials remain as green plants throughout the winter. There are short-lived and long-lived perennials.

Traditionally used in formal borders, perennials are used more frequently now in mixed borders with small shrubs and trees, in island beds where they mix well with ornamental grasses and can be enjoyed from all sides, in naturalistic gardens with other native plants and in containers. Determine the position of the perennial in the bed by the height of the foliage, not the flower which may be of short duration. For impact, arrange the groupings in sweeps or masses: the smaller the plant, the larger the number of plants within a grouping.

Bulbs

Bulbs are used for seasonal effects in mass plantings or individually in beds and borders. You can choose bulbs to add color to the garden in spring, summer or fall, bulbs to plant in containers outdoors or in colder climates, or bulbs that can be brought to flower indoors in winter. Some bulbs lend themselves to planting in meadows and woodlands where they take on a wild, natural look demanding little future care.

Herbs, Vegetables and Fruits

Herbs are grown for culinary and medicinal purposes. Flowers, leaves and seeds are used for their decorative qualities and fragrance in the garden and for potpourris.

Vegetables and fruits are plants grown for their edible roots, stalks, leaves, ovaries, flowers or seeds.

Herbs, vegetables and fruits can be isolated in specialized gardens where they are easiest to handle if you are growing many of them. They can also be incorporated into beds and borders. Many have decorative foliage (fennel, sage, lettuce, parsley, asparagus, strawberries), flowers (comfrey, squash and zucchini, dwarf crabapples) and fruits (blueberries, dwarf fruit trees) which warrant their inclusion in mixed plantings. Many are suitable for containers (thyme, sage, hyssop, dwarf tomatoes, strawberries, fruit trees).

Chapter 3

Soil

Good Garden Soil

Good garden soil is essential for a successful garden. To be ideal, garden soil should satisfy the basic needs of plants for nutrients, moisture and air. Soil must be loosely structured to permit easy access by plant roots to nutrients and air, while striking the right balance between good drainage and retaining sufficient moisture to allow roots time to absorb it.

Few gardeners will find their soil ideal. Compacted and overly dry or overly moist soils may restrict plant growth. The absence of necessary minerals may set up a chemical imbalance, keeping some nutrients unavailable. Healthy, fertile soil contains the obvious earthworms and the invisible microscopic bacteria and other organisms that work beneath the soil surface to break down organic material. Under ideal conditions, mineral particles, also present in the soil, work together with available moisture and air to provide conditions hospitable to promote plant life. Good soil holds nutrients and moisture, benefiting plants during times of drought. There are a number of steps, outlined below, that you can take to prepare and improve poor soil for planting.

For further information about soil testing and other local gardening needs and problems, call the agricultural agent at your local county office of the cooperative extension service. There is an office in every county of every state. This service is listed under the U.S. Government, Department of Agriculture, as Cooperative Extension, Extension or under the county name (i.e., Jones County Extension) in the telephone book. Or call your state land-grant university soil testing lab. Many garden centers provide this service. You can also buy a do-it-yourself kit with instructions, but home-use kits are not as reliable as agricultural agents.

Soil Preparation

Soil preparation includes testing the soil for its pH balance and nutrient levels, checking for drainage, working the soil to a depth of 8 to 12 inches by hand or with a rototiller and adding any necessary soil amendments. Mulching after planting will help keep your soil in good condition.

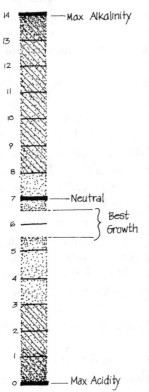

Adjusting soil pH. A soil test will determine the pH level of your soil. Changing the pH of the soil, if indicated, to a rating between 6 and 7, and maintaining it there, will insure that nitrogen, phosphorus and potassium will be available to most plants. A soil test will also reveal the levels of nitrogen, potassium, phosphorus and other trace elements present or lacking in your soil.

To raise pH, add lime (ground or dolomitic limestone). To lower pH, add sulfur, iron sulfate, aluminum sulfate, acid-reacting fertilizer, sawdust or peat moss.

Testing for drainage. Fill a planting hole with water. Water should empty out of a well-drained hole in 10 minutes. If water leaves a hole too quickly, add humus to the soil to make it more moisture retentive. If it takes 30 minutes or more for the hole to empty, the soil requires correction. In areas that are seasonally wet, that have shallow soil or have a high water table, plant high by mounding soil under the plants to raise them slightly above the existing soil level, or plant in raised beds. In severely wet situations, it may be necessary to install drainage tiles or perforated pipes set in gravel to collect and carry the groundwater to lower areas, or to change the grading to divert surface water away from your plants. If the growing conditions cannot be satisfactorily modified, choose plants that tolerate damp soil.

Amending soil structure. You can amend your soil structure by adding and incorporating bulk materials to improve bacterial activity and nutrient levels, drainage and structure. Soil amendments can be organic or inorganic.

Organic amendments are used mainly for flower and shrub borders and vegetable gardens where they are should be worked into the entire planting bed for the best results. Do not enrich individual holes. They may behave like containers, encouraging roots to remain within the planting area rather than reaching out into the surrounding soil and becoming well established.

Organic amendments include compost, leaf mold, peat moss, animal manure, grass clippings, agricultural and wood by-products, and converted city sludge (the organic portion of urban trash collections). Organic materials help increase the soil's ability to hold moisture and maintain good soil structure while adding nutrients. They are a temporary solution as they eventually break down, but they provide necessary nutrients and structure to get plants off to a good start.

Several inches of shredded leaves and aged manure can be spread on shrub and flower borders during fall cleanup to act as mulch, protecting the plant roots and soil surface from compaction during the winter. Amendments can be spread on the soil surface of the vegetable garden after the last harvest, worked in or left to continue decomposing with the weather. In spring any unacceptable residues can be removed to the compost heap.

Compost is decomposed garden debris. For a discussion of compost, see Chapter 7.

Leaf mold is partially decomposed leaves and can be acidic when made of oak leaves. It can be worked into your soil or used as mulch.

Peat moss is partially decayed sphagnum moss mined from swamps. It has no nutritive value in itself but does retain moisture, nutrients and air. It is quite acidic.

Animal manures (cow, horse, pig, chicken and other fowl) should be composted and well-aged, or left to winter in the soil, as they may burn plant roots if used fresh. They are usually worked into the soil, but strawy manure can be used as mulch.

Raw wood by-products (ground bark, sawdust) can be neutralized with the addition of nitrogen. Otherwise, the bacteria that cause the decomposing process will draw nitrogen from the soil. Fine-textured wood by-products are added to compost piles or worked into the soil. Heavily textured ones are used as mulch.

Grass clippings should be composted first if they have gone to seed.

Inorganic amendments, including sand and gypsum (calcium sulfate), change the physical structure of soil. They are added to heavy clay soils to aerate and lighten them. They help break up clods and improve drainage. Use coarse *builder's sand* which tends to stay mixed into the soil. Finer sand rises to the surface or adheres to clay particles producing an even heavier substance (adobe). *Gypsum* is added to soil to reduce saltiness. In particular, it can eliminate the burning effects of runoff from winter highway salts. *Vermiculite* and *perlite* are inert, extremely light particles used to aerate soils. Because of their high cost, they are only practical for use in potting soils in containers.

Work the soil only after it has dried out sufficiently following winter or a heavy, drenching rain. Otherwise, you may compact the soil, causing a breakdown of the structure. This is especially true with clay soils. If you plant seeds and seedlings in soil that is too wet, they may rot.

Whenever possible, prepare the soil well in advance of a major planting, as much as a full season, so that it can settle. If you cannot, then prepare the soil at least a week or two in advance of planting. Newly worked beds may have soil that is too fluffy. Plants will sink unevenly into such soil. If you must plant immediately, tamp down newly turned and amended soil by treading lightly across the entire cultivated area. If the soil is overly dry and hard, soak it with a sprinkler a day in advance to soften before digging or weeding. Mulch newly prepared beds heavily to control compaction and weeds until you are ready to plant; then only a light cultivation, if any, will be necessary.

Chapter 4

How to Choose Plants

In most areas, plants can be purchased locally although choices may be limited. Select plants from a reliable source, preferably plants grown in your region to insure hardiness and adaptability to your climate and soil. Always buy nursery-grown stock (not collected plants) and make sure the nursery or garden center gives a guarantee; when the nursery installs a major tree or shrub, the standard guarantee is for one year. Buy the largest plant you can afford so you will have a show the first year.

Ordering by mail broadens your choice of plants and assures you of a supply should your local sources fail to have what you want. Purchasing mail-order stock can be a gamble unless you check carefully to insure that your choices are hardy and will do well in your area. Sizes will be limited by shipping limitations. Mail-order plants may take more than one growing season to reach an effective size or to bloom. (See the appendix titled "Ordering and Caring for Mail-Order Plants.")

Do not buy plants collected in the wild. Many native plants are on the endangered list. Fortunately, many nurseries now specialize in native trees and shrubs and wildflowers that have been propagated from seed. Nursery-propagated plants are easier to establish in the garden than collected ones.

Understanding the plant label. Plants are classified according to an internationally accepted binomial system. Each category is progressively more specific.

A well-labeled plant will give the following information: generic name, which is always capitalized and italicized or underlined, followed by a specific epithet, or species name, which is always in lower case. A genus is made up of plants that are closely related with similar characteristics. A species consists of a group of plants that are interfertile and breed true. Hybrids (crosses between different species or varieties) are possible in nature but rare. When applicable, the binomial may be followed by a subspecies or Latin variety (*var.*) name. Variety names are not capitalized but are italicized or underlined. The final category may be a cultivar name, which is preceded by "cv." or enclosed in single quotes. Cultivar names are never italicized or underlined.

A variety is a group of plants occurring naturally in the wild which resembles, in most characteristics, other members of the same species but differs in some significant way such as ultimate size, leaf shape or flower color. A cultivar also resembles other species members but again differs in one or more significant characteristics. People generally play a part in the development of a cultivar, which comes about by controlled hybridization, or from selection under cultivation. A cultivar may also derive in nature from an abnormal individual plant. Cultivars are maintained in cultivation by vegetative propagation (i.e., cuttings, divisions) or by selection. An "x" in a plant name means that the plant is a cross between two or more species. *Viburnum x pragense* (Prague Viburnum) is a cross between *Viburnum rhytidophyllum* and *Viburnum utile*.

For example, *Viburnum plicatum* var. *tomentosum* cv. Mariesii. *Viburnum* is the genus, *plicatum* the species, *tomentosum* the variety and Mariesii the cultivar. Its common name is Mariesii Double File Viburnum. It is an elegant white flowering shrub, 8 by l0 feet, horizontally growing, wider at maturity than it is tall, with reddish purple fall foliage. It is spectacular in bloom characterized by snow-white flat-topped blooms that march double file above the foliage on the outwardly spreading branches. In late summer, berries turn from bright red to black and are favored by birds. Fall foliage is reddish purple.

The genus *Viburnum* is a valuable group of shrubs, consisting of many other outstanding, but very different, garden plants. By knowing the correct botanical name, you will be able to choose the one that best suits your needs for growth habit and ornamental interest. For instance, if you want an upright plant, you might choose a cultivar of *V. dilatatum* (Linden Viburnum), 8 to 10 feet, with creamy white, flat-topped blossoms and cherry-red fruits. Other species and hybrids include *V. carlesii* (Koreanspice Viburnum), 4 to 8 feet and *V. x burkwoodii* (Burkwood Viburnum), 8 to 10 feet, compact growers which are outstanding for their fragrant, snowball-shaped bloom. *V. setigerum* (Tea Viburnum), 8 to 12 feet, is a leggy plant, useful in the back of the border, with clusters of bright red, long-lasting fruit in late fall. There is an evergreen variety, *V. rhytidophyllum* (Leatherleaf Viburnum), 10 to 15 feet, that blends well with needle and other broadleaf evergreens in a background planting.

A genus listing followed by "sp." or "spp." (species, singular and plural) indicates that there are a number of valuable members within that genus or group. This is common among shrubs and perennials.

Buy or order plants from a reliable source that labels them by botanical name, as common names vary greatly from region to region, leading to confusion. Some labels will even include basic planting and cultural information as well as design considerations.

At the nursery or garden center, plants are sold as follows: Trees, shrubs and some perennials are sold bare-root, balled- and-burlaped (B & B) or in containers. A bare-root plant is sold in a dormant condition and is available only in winter or early spring. A balled-and-burlaped plant is grown in a field, dug out in spring or late fall when the plant is not in active growth and the root ball wrapped in burlap to keep the soil intact and to protect the roots from drying out. A container-grown plant is grown in a plastic or metal container, which keeps the root system intact so it can be transplanted in any season provided it has time to become established in its new location before the ground freezes. Small plants, including annuals, vegetable and herb seedlings, are sold in plastic pots or market packs available during the planting season.

Trees

Trees are commonly sold balled-and-burlaped. Large trees are sold B & B or in wire baskets. Smaller trees may also be available either bare-root or container-grown.

Large shade trees are sold by caliper (a measurement of the diameter of the trunk 1 foot above soil level, i.e., 2½ inches caliper, 4 inches caliper, etc.). Smaller trees and evergreens are frequently measured by height: 6 to 8 feet, 10 to 12 feet, etc.

Choose a tree with a vertical, well-balanced, and even branching habit and a dominant main leader (growing tip of the trunk). The destruction of the leader can produce a deformed crown in trees. Look for a balance between the top, or head, and the root ball, as a well-balanced tree will establish more readily. Field-grown trees will have their side branches pruned back heavily. Avoid a top-heavy tree with a small root ball. Check the root system; it should be evenly developed and symmetrical. Avoid a tree with kinked or encircling roots visible on the soil surface. Encircling roots will continue to grow around the plant, eventually girdling and killing it.

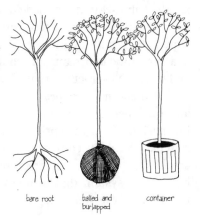

bare root   balled and   container
burlapped

Check the trunk, particularly at ground level, for damage from mowers or weedeaters in the nursery, and the main branches for signs of past or more recent damage. A healthy tree will have a straight, upright trunk and healthy well-formed branches. If the tree is in leaf, foliage should appear clean and fresh. Leaf color should be dark and even, not scorched, yellowed, mildewed, spotted or chewed. Cracked bark dieback of branch tips, small holes drilled in the bark of the trunk or main branches, oozing sap and discoloration or deformity of buds, leaves or branches are all signs of insect and disease problems.

Stake large trees against strong winds for a year while the roots become established. Mulch all trees well after planting to control moisture loss. Protect the bark of young trees from sunscald and winter rodent damage with burlap or tree wrap, which can be purchased in rolls from garden supply sources. Protect tree trunks from mowing machine damage by incorporating them in a planting bed or surrounding them with a circle of mulch.

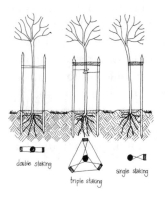

double staking

triple staking   single staking

Bare-root. Bare-root trees are less expensive than either container-grown or balled-and-burlaped ones. Select a bare-root tree as soon as this stock is available in the nurseries. Fruit trees are commonly sold bare-root. Plant a bare-root tree within a day or two of purchase, or pack the roots carefully in moist peat moss, leaf mold or sawdust and set it in the shade until it can be planted. A bare-root tree can also be stored "heeled in" (buried up to the tips) in a trench and kept damp and cool for several weeks. Never let the roots dry out.

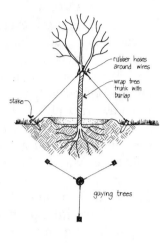

Balled-and-burlaped. Plant balled-and-burlaped trees whenever available but preferably in the spring or fall. The root ball should be compact and firm, not cracked or broken. (A firm root ball indicates a well-developed fibrous root system that is able to support the tree.) Until planting time, shade the tree; keep the root ball moist by carefully watering

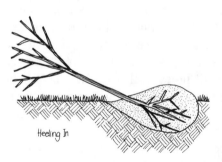

Heeling In

with a slow hose from the top, and occasionally spray the foliage to refresh it. Spraying the foliage with a moisture-loss retardant will cut moisture loss through the leaves.

Container-grown. Plant container-grown trees, as available duringq the growing season. Containers can be metal, plastic or wood. For trees, containers are measured in inches: 24 inches, 36 inches or larger.

Check that a staked tree has a strong trunk; untie it and make sure it is straight and doesn't flop. A container-grown tree should not have roots that encircle the surface of the container or come out of the drainage hole, indicating that the tree is root-bound, or too big for the container. Until planting time, either set the container in the shade or cover it with peat moss or soil. Keep the root ball moist and occasionally spray the foliage, or spray with a moisture-retardant as suggested for balled-and-burlaped plants.

Shrubs

Shrubs are commonly sold by group size (10 to 12 inches, 12 to 15 inches, 15 to 18 inches, etc.) or in one-, two-, five-, seven-, fifteen- (or larger) gallon containers, but they may also be purchased balled-and-burlaped or bare-root. Select a shrub with a well-balanced branching habit and even form. Reject a plant with blunt, stubbly pruned ends or crossing branches, which invite insects and diseases.

cover bare roots
with soil or leaves

Bare-root. As with trees, bare-root shrubs are less expensive than container-grown and balled-and-burlaped plants, but they are available only when dormant. Choose a shrub with firm roots that radiate out from the main root evenly and at different levels to anchor the plant and ensure symmetrical growth. Do not allow roots to dry out. Plant as soon as possible and before growth begins.

Balled-and-burlaped. Plant balled-and-burlaped shrubs when available but preferably in the spring or fall. Look for a firm, compact ball indicating a well-developed fibrous root system. Do not choose a shrub with a dry, cracked or loose root ball. Push your finger into the top several inches of dirt near the trunk to see whether it has encircling or kinked roots which may strangle the plant or inhibit its growth. Until you are ready to plant it, shade the shrub, keep the soil moist and spray the foliage occasionally.

Container-grown. A container-grown shrub should be well anchored in its container. To test, lift it carefully by the trunk. If the soil moves easily, the shrub probably has an underdeveloped root system and has been moved recently from a smaller container. Conversely, if there is a thick mass of roots visible on the soil surface and around the edge of the root ball, the plant has been in the container too long and may be root-bound and unable to recover when you transplant it. Reject a plant in a rusted, split or disintegrating container. Until planting time, shade the container because hot sun will heat up the roots, especially in a metal can. Keep the root ball moist and spray the foliage occasionally.

Perennials, Biennials and Annuals

Some perennials are sold bare-root or balled-and-burlaped, but most are sold in pots or containers. Annuals and biennals are sold in pots or market packs. Choose healthy looking plants with clean, fresh foliage. Stems should be short and thick. Tall, lanky plants will have weak root systems. Avoid plants that have heavily wilted, yellow or discolored foliage, whose roots have grown out of the container, or plants with root balls that have dried out. Selecting plants that are in bloom reassures you that you are getting the color you want. However, a blooming plant may have an underdeveloped root system that may not be able to support it after transplanting. Remove the blossoms at planting time to allow the plant to establish well. Inspect all plants for insects and diseases.

Bulbs

Bulbs should be firm and unblemished and should feel heavy for their size. The heaviness assures you that they have not dried out during storage.

Chapter 5

Plant Care

How to Plant and Transplant

Once you have selected a plant and prepared the planting site, you must plant correctly to assure that your purchase gets off to a healthy start.

In general, if you are planting a large number of plants, prepare the entire planting site in advance and allow the soil to rest for seven to ten days, or for as long as an entire season before planting. If the planting area has dried out, soak the soil well several days ahead of time to make digging easier. Unless otherwise directed, set plants at the same level at which they were growing in the nursery or in their containers. There is usually a visible soil line on the stem. With multi-stemmed shrubs and perennials, set the crown of the plant, the spot where the stems or leafy top and the roots of the plant meet, at the same depth. If set too deep, the plant will drown. If set too shallow, the plant will dry out.

Water in thoroughly, using a slow trickle from a hose, until the soil is loose and muddy. This will eliminate air pockets.

Trees and Shrubs

Bare-root. Plant these as soon as the soil is workable. Soak roots for several hours in tepid water before planting and prune any damaged roots or canes. Make a mound of soil in the center of a prepared hole and spread the roots over the mound. Start adding soil carefully. Water well when the hole is two-thirds filled. Finish filling the hole and firm the soil gently around roots. Water again. Mound loose soil around the stem up to the lowest branch to protect the stem and to steady the plant until it is established and has leafed out. Then carefully remove excess soil and spread mulch.

Balled-and-burlaped. Check the soil level on nursery-grown trees. If the trunk appears to rise straight out of the soil ball, scratch down around the base of the trunk to find that spot where the roots begin to flare out from the trunk. You may find several inches of excess soil covering the ball. Remove it before planting to arrive at the correct planting level. Measure the size of the root ball; do not guess. Place a piece of burlap to the side of the hole to hold the soil. Dig a hole twice as wide as

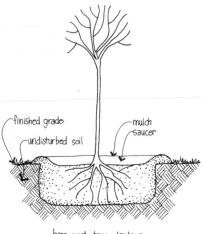

bare root tree planting

the root ball and the same depth of the root ball (or a little shallower since a heavy plant may sink slightly). Lift the plant by grasping the burlap and cord, not the stem or trunk (which may tear the roots). Carefully set the plant in the hole. Stand back to check the placement. Is the plant straight? Cut away cords, and tuck the burlap down into the planting hole where it will rot away. Remove (entirely) any plastic cords or wrappings, which will not rot.

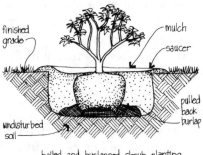

balled and burlapped shrub planting

Backfill the hole, lightly tamping down the soil with your foot or shovel as you go. Build a shallow saucer of soil around the base of the plant to hold water.

Container-grown. Dampen the root ball in advance to free the roots and soil so you will be able to lift the plant out of the container; otherwise, cut the container down both sides. Dig a hole wider than the container. Measure the container or root ball to check for proper depth. Check the root ball; cut encircling roots; untangle and spread out matted roots. When the hole is partially filled, water to eliminate air pockets. Fill the rest of the hole and pack soil gently. Water again and mulch. Trim out any damaged or crossing branches.

Transplanting. Using a sharp spade, dig as large a root ball as possible. Lift and carry small plants on the spade. Tip large plants to one side of the hole, push a wad of burlap down one side and pull it under them and around the ball. Wrap and tie the root ball securely. Lift the plant out onto a piece of plastic or cardboard and slide it to the new location. Minimize transplanting shock by moving plants when dormant and on a cloudy day. Before digging, spray leafy plants with an antidesiccant to reduce moisture loss from the leaves. After transplanting, keep root systems moist, mist foliage and water. Prune away any damaged branches.

Perennials and Annuals

Transplant perennials and annuals from their containers before they become top-heavy or begin blooming. Plant in newly prepared areas or add plants to existing beds. Dig a spacious hole for each plant and space at recommended intervals. Moisten the transplants before removing them from the container. Run a knife around the inside of the rim and tap the container sharply on a hard surface. Turn the plant out into the palm of your hand with the stem between your fingers so you can catch and retain as much soil as possible. Gently break up the outer edges of the dirt ball, loosening any encircling roots at the bottom and side surfaces by pulling them gently away from the soil mass and spreading them out in a hole large enough not to cramp them. If the plant has been started in a soilless mix, shake off as much as possible to encourage the roots to move out into new soil. Unless otherwise instructed, set each plant at the same soil level at which it was growing before, especially those growing from a crown, such as pansies, campanulas, astilbe and hosta. Firm the soil gently and soak each plant—especially seedlings and plants with small root balls—with a 10 percent solution of water-soluble fertilizer or manure tea. Pinch back top growth to encourage root growth and bushiness. Plant on overcast days when possible and shade young plants from direct sun (or late frosts) for several days. Use baskets, planting trays or newspapers.

For information on digging and dividing perennials, see Chapter 13.

Bulbs

If you are planting a large number of bulbs, excavate the entire area, digging deeper than planting depth. Improve drainage, if necessary, by spreading a 2- to 3-inch layer of gravel or sharp sand. Add a thin layer of soil. Enrich poor soil by mixing in well-rotted organic material and a slow-release bulb food, 5-10-10, or superphosphate. Level the bottom of the excavation, set the bulbs and carefully cover with the remaining enriched soil. For a planting of mixed bulbs, set those requiring the greatest depth first, add a level of soil, then set those bulbs needing shallower planting next.

If you are planting bulbs in individual holes in an existing bed, insure good drainage by adding fine gravel or sharp sand at the bottom of the planting hole. Add a layer of compost, or other organic matter, before planting. Add a commercial bulb fertilizer or superphosphate toward the bottom of each planting hole where roots can easily reach it; mix it in well to prevent direct contact with the bulb.

If you are planting in containers, the same principles apply. Bulbs can be closely planted as long as they do not touch each other or the side of the pot.

If you have rodent problems, bulbs can be planted in a raised bed lined with chicken wire. Or you can encircle small groups of bulbs with wire cages in the ground before covering with soil. A gritty, gravelly soil also deters rodents from digging.

Space and set bulbs at the depth recommended for each variety (measuring from the bottom of the bulb). As a general rule, large bulbs should be planted about twice their depth, smaller bulbs slightly deeper than twice their depth. In heavy clay soil, plant bulbs slightly shallower and in light sandy soil or in very dry places a little deeper.

Set the bulb into the soil with growing tip up, and the basal plate, from which the roots will grow, down. A bulb planted wrong-side-up will sprout and find the surface but with added difficulty. When in doubt, plant the bulb on its side.

For tall-growing bulbs requiring stakes (dahlia, lily, gladiolus), set the stakes at planting time to avoid damaging future root systems.

After planting, water thoroughly and deeply to settle the soil. Mulch the bed well to reduce moisture loss and deter weeds.

For further discussion on bulbs, see Chapter 11.

Water Lilies and Other Aquatic Plants

Wait until late spring for the water temperature to reach 70° F. In a pail or basket, plant aquatic plants in a soil mix (3 parts heavy clay and 1 part dehydrated cow manure). Cover the soil surface with ¹/₂ inch of gravel to weight it down. Set the container in the pool with the soil surface 6 to 12 inches below the water's surface. If the pool is very deep, create a platform for the container out of concrete blocks or bricks. Hardy water lilies and lotus are perennials that may remain in outdoor pools all year. Tropical water lilies are annuals and should be pulled and composted at the end of the season. Plan to renew the soil in the containers every second year.

For information on planting containers and hanging baskets, see Chapter 9.

For information on seeding and sodding a lawn, see Chapter 6.

How to Prune

Pruning restricts or directs the growth of plants. Pruning controls size and shape and maintains plant health. You will need to prune heavily only to remove dead, diseased, damaged, structurally weak or crossing branches. (Crossing branches are part of the natural growth habit of cotoneaster, quince and white forsythia [*Abeliophyllum distzchum*] and can be left.)

Plants are pruned to enhance their natural form or winter silhouette and to reveal colorful and decorative bark. When you prune for a natural or informal look, always bear in mind the appearance and typical growth pattern of each species.

Plants are pruned to perform specific functions: to provide shade (trees), define garden spaces (hedges) or create special effects which give a more decorative or formal look (topiary, espalier).

Some special circumstances: For safety in areas of high winds or heavy snow falls, thin heavily canopied trees or large shrubs. In years

Pruning:
at a 45° angle
just above an
outward facing
lateral bud

of drought, thin heavily foliaged plants to cut back on water consumption and transpiration. For safety, remove thick undergrowth to reduce hazards from brush fires during periods of abnormal dryness.

Plants may need heavy top or root pruning to stimulate new growth, to renew an overgrown, poorly flowering plant or to increase fruit and nut production.

Water sprouts and sucker growth—abnormal, sometimes rapidly growing, small branches that usually do not follow the pattern of the plant—can be removed at any time.

Pruning Techniques

Pruning involves two major techniques: heading back and thinning out. These techniques produce different results. Many pruning situations require both methods. Other techniques that control plant growth include pinching back, limbing up and root pruning.

Heading back creates a dense formal look and keeps plants lower and narrower. In this procedure, part of a shoot or branch is cut back, but not as far as the point where it joins another branch or trunk. Removing the end of a branch causes multiple branching out behind or at the point of the cut, thickening the plant. Always cut just above a lateral bud (side bud on a plant stem) to avoid long stubs. New growth will follow the direction of the bud, so choosing a bud pointing outward discourages crossing branches. Heading back is used for hedges and topiaries and to thicken young plants.

Electric shearing is a heading-back technique often used to keep a plant "in bounds." It can result in a garden of crowded, stiff, rounded or upside-down pyramidal shapes. A more attractive solution can be achieved by replacing the overgrown

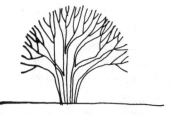

Pruning: Heading Back

plants with more suitable varieties whose mature size and shape suit the sites. Overpruning destroys the natural habit and identity of any plant.

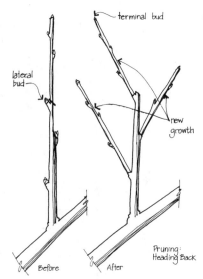

Thinning out enhances and maintains the natural shape of the plant. In this procedure, an entire shoot or branch is cut back to a branch point, the place where it joins another branch. Do not cut an overly extended branch off even with the plant's outline, but selectively thin by "deep pruning"—reaching into the plant's interior and removing the whole branch back to a main branch or trunk within the plant silhouette. This opens up the plant to air and light. Growth will continue from the terminal bud at the end of the remaining branch or trunk. Thinning reduces the number of new shoots from lateral buds, inhibits branching and allows limbs to grow longer. Thinning is used for shade trees, fruit trees and shrubs, especially flowering varieties.

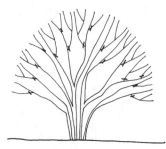

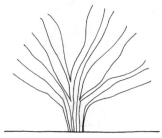

Pruning: Thinning Out

Pinching and *shearing back* are forms of heading back in which you remove part of the current season's growth, or the growing point (terminal or leaf bud), by pinching it out by hand or by shearing at regular intervals during the growing season. These techniques result in thicker plants and promote plant vigor. When used to remove flower buds (chrysanthemums and asters), they delay blooming. Use pinching and shearing back to control shrubs, perennials and annuals, including herbs.

Limbing up, or removing the lower branches, of trees and shrubs allows more light into heavily shaded areas

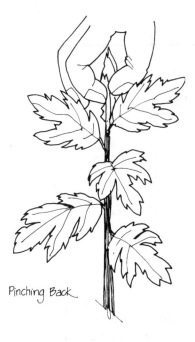

Pinching Back

and increases air circulation. It creates head and mowing room under large shade trees.

Rejuvenation aids overgrown plants. Thin out old wood over a three-year period to rejuvenate a plant. Cut one-third of old thick stems at the base each year just before the spring growth spurt and remove all dead and twiggy branchlets. Or cut deciduous shrubs to the ground and let them start again. New growth will be rapid.

Root pruning stimulates growth or prepares large plants for transplanting. Dig a circle around the plant approximately 1 foot out from the trunk for each inch of trunk caliper. (Caliper, a measurement of the diameter of the tree trunk, is taken 6 inches above the ground line for trees up to 4 inches in diameter and at 1 foot above ground line for larger trees.)

For instance, a tree with a 4-inch caliper should have a 4-foot circle cut around it. The depth of the cut will vary with the species but should be deep enough to cut through the feeder roots of the plant. This encourages the plant to develop a thick mass of new feeder roots within the root ball to replace those that will be severed when the plant is moved. Root prune the season before transplanting, leaving the bottom roots intact until the final root ball is dug.

Root pruning is also practiced to keep a plant that tends to "sucker," or send up new shoots outside the boundaries of the original plant, in bounds (shrub dogwoods, some deciduous hollies, Carolina allspice,

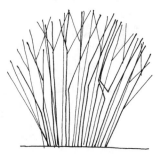

rejuvenation

kerria). Again, cut a circle around the plant, cutting through any roots that connect the suckers to the main plant and remove root and sucker. This is useful in controlling shrubs as well as perennials that spread out beyond the space you wish to allot to them. Suckers with attached roots can be planted to propagate new plants.

Why and When to Prune

Major, or heavy, pruning is best carried out in late winter when plants are dormant and leaf fall has revealed branching habits, which simplifies the task. The temperature should be above freezing. Minor, or light pruning (minimal cutting of woody growth, damaged or dead branches or excessive foliage on established plants) can be done at any time of the year. Always use clean sharp tools to perform any pruning task.

If you suspect your plant has a disease, sterilize blades between each cut with a mild 10 percent alcohol solution.

Shade trees. Thinning of a tree crown, the uppermost canopy of the tree, should be done in winter when the tree is dormant, or in late summer when new wood has hardened off. Thinning reduces the load, lessens the possibility of storm damage and falling limbs and allows more light to reach the area beneath. Branches overhanging roofs, walkways, pools, decks or other trafficked areas should be removed for head clearance and safety. This particularly applies to brittle- or soft-wooded trees. Any pruning of major trees should be carried out by professionals. Although it requires time and is costly, thinning results in a healthy long-lived plant.

Ornamental trees. Many specimen trees, deciduous and evergreen, can be allowed to develop naturally. You need only prune away damaged, crossing or diseased branches, or modify excessive height or spreading form.

Some ornamentals may need training as young plants to develop a straight central leader and strong lateral branches to form the main scaffold of the mature tree. When the tree is young, select a strong upwardly growing branch to become the central leader. Remove all other branches that grow too closely together or that form narrow crotch angles to the main trunk. Continue to prune back secondary branches and water sprouts. Limb up, or remove the lower branches, gradually as the tree develops to attain the desired head height, the distance from the ground to the first branches, keeping at least two thirds of the foliage at all times for proper photosynthesis for a strong tree.

Multistemmed trees. Nursery-grown stock is frequently pruned to have a single trunk, but some types of trees (maple, birch, deciduous magnolia, hazel, franklinia) naturally develop into multistemmed or shrub-like forms, attractive alternatives to a garden of single-trunk trees. Care should be given to these plants to encourage their natural growth habit. Choose three or more strongly growing, slightly outward leaning stems to become the eventual trunks of the tree. As the plant develops, gradually limb up these trunks and thin out any crossing branches or excessive upper twiggy growth.

Needle evergreen trees and shrubs. Prune needle evergreen trees and shrubs to maintain their size, compactness and balance, preferably just before a growth spurt so new cuts will be covered quickly. Pine and spruce have one growth period, which is in spring. Arborvitae, hemlock, juniper and yew have a second spurt in midsummer and may require a second trimming. Do not prune in early fall since new growth stimulated by pruning will not have time to harden off before winter.

Prune conifers (cone-bearing trees) back to visible live buds. Cutting behind those buds will result in stubs as most conifers will not produce new growth. Only hemlocks, some yews, retinospora and arborvitae will put out growth from dormant buds on old wood.

If a conifer accidentally loses its leader, train a new one by tying a lower side shoot to the remaining stub, or create a splint by tying a light stake to the main leader below the break and a side shoot to the splint above.

Limit the yearly growth of pines and promote bushiness by pinching out, or shearing back, one half to two thirds of the new growth (called "candles"), each spring before needles develop along the candles.

Needle evergreens lose their lower branches when they are shaded out and will not grow new ones. To prevent heavy loss of lower limbs, you can thin out thickly planted stands of conifers and cut back upper limbs to allow more light to reach lower ones.

For a natural look when pruning any needle evergreen trees or shrubs, such as yew or juniper often used as ground covers, lift up an upper branch for better visibility. Deep prune the overly extended branch below by cutting it back several inches or more within the contours of the shrub. This will avoid a sheared look and hide pruning cuts.

Hedges. You should trim so that the top of the hedge is narrower than the bottom, admitting light to the base of the plant and reducing dieback of bottom branches. Prune deciduous hedges in late winter by shearing with clippers to create a dense formal look. Prune broadleaf and needle evergreen hedges by hand in early spring, just before a growth spurt, so that new cuts will be quickly covered. (Electric shearing destroys the foliage of broadleaf evergreens.)

Spring-blooming shrubs. These plants flower on wood formed the previous year. Prune, if necessary, as they finish blooming and before they begin forming next year's flower buds. Prune to enhance their natural shape. Spring-bloomers include azalea, alternate-leaf butterfly-bush (*Buddleia alternifolia*), forsythia, bigleaf and oakleaf hydrangea, mock orange, quince, rhododendron, Vanhoutte spirea (*Spiraea* x *vanhouttei*) and winter jasmine.

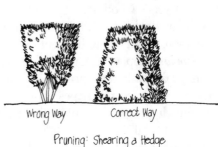

Wrong Way   Correct Way

Pruning: Shearing a Hedge

Summer-blooming shrubs. These plants flower on wood produced during the same growing season. Prune in late winter to encourage summer flower buds and to enhance the natural shape. Some summer-bloomers are abelia, althea, butterfly bush (*Buddleia davidii*), caryopteris, callicarpa, crape myrtle, smoothleaf hydrangea (*Hydrangea arborescens*), panicle hydrangea (*H. paniculata*), hypericum, shrub rose, Bumald spirea (*Spiraea* x *bumalda*) and vitex.

Container-grown and *bare-root plants.* Container-grown trees and shrubs do not need pruning at planting time other than to remove any damaged roots or branches. Bare-root plants do need pruning. Remove as much as one-third to one-half of the top growth to compensate for root loss and to encourage new growth after the roots have become established. This work can be done as long as a month or more after planting.

Overgrown plants. Prune in late winter just before the spring growth spurt and when plant structure is not obscured by leaves. Thin out old wood over a three-year period to rejuvenate a plant. For shrubs, cut one-third of old thick stems at the base each year and remove all dead and twiggy branchlets. Or, cut deciduous shrubs to within 2 to 3 inches of the ground and let them start again. If the tree or shrub is a spring-bloomer, you will sacrifice the flowers, but only for the next season. New growth will be rapid since the mature root system will put all of its energy into the production of new wood.

Vines. Deciduous and evergreen vines need occasional pruning. Thinning and trimming is important to keep rampant vines within bounds or to reveal interesting branch structure, leaf silhouettes or colorful bark. Individual vines, especially clematis, may have special requirements. Vines bloom on the previous year's wood, current season's wood in summer or on both old and current season's growth. Prune vines that bloom on the previous year's wood after they bloom—those that bloom on current season's wood, before they bloom. Check with your local garden center or mail-order nursery to find out how your vine blooms.

Topiary. Topiary is made by shaping and training twiggy plants (boxwood, Japanese hollies, privet, yew) into fanciful shapes (birds, foxes, dogs) or architectural shapes (domes, pyramids or pillars). It requires constant clipping and pruning. Since topiary needs the full distribution of sunlight for uniform growth, maintain the top narrower than the bottom to admit light to the bottom of the plant.

Espaliers. Espaliers are trees or shrubs of essentially two-dimensional form, trained to grow in one plane—flat against a supporting wall, fence or trellis and confined to a small space. In northern climates, New England or the Pacific Northwest, fruit trees trained against a south-facing wall benefit from the reflected heat. East- or west-facing walls are better for espaliers in hotter climates where reflected heat in summer from a south-facing wall can burn plants.

Espaliers can be trained in various patterns, from loose informal styles to more complex single cordon (the main stem growing vertically with matching side branches growing horizontally or at 45° angles) and multiarmed, U-shaped candelabras.

To start a new espalier, remove the rear and front branches of the plant. Spread and fasten remaining young flexible branches against their support system. Pinch or prune out surplus shoots as they appear, as frequently as every month during the growing season. Keep tightly trimmed and nip out terminal buds when the espalier reaches proper width and height. Further major pruning and training is mostly done in the spring, just before a growth spurt when twigs and branches are pliable, and again in midsummer. Spring-flowering plants should be pruned after bloom. Never allow the ties to become too tight and girdle the limb. *Fruit trees, grapevines and berry bushes.* Training of young plants is necessary to develop strong enough branching frameworks to bear the weight of the fruit, to achieve leaf growth for maximum exposure to the sun and for ease of harvesting. Pruning is carried out in mid- to late-winter when plants are dormant in order to encourage new growth and fruit production and to balance and distribute the fruit load. Fruiting habits and cultural requirements vary among specific varieties.

How to Fertilize

Understanding the Fertilizer Label

There are two kinds of fertilizer: organic (natural) and inorganic, or synthetic (chemical). Organic fertilizers, including compost, leaf mold, aged manure, bone meal and blood meal, are used to enrich the soil, improve its texture and provide nitrogen, phosphorus and potassium as well as other trace elements. They supply a slow, steady diet but have the disadvantage of being bulky and, therefore, hard to work with and hard to store.

Aged manure can be "brewed" to make a manure tea. Add several inches of aged or dehydrated manure to a pail of water. Allow the mixture to sit for several hours and apply as a liquid fertilizer. Easier to apply than other bulky organic fertilizers, use it for watering seedlings and small transplants, and in the vegetable garden to feed crops during the growing season.

Synthetic fertilizers are easier to find, store and use. They come in many formulas and forms: liquid, powder and granules. Except in the case of "slow-release" fertilizer, the nutrients are readily available and are designed for rapid absorption into the plant. Water-soluble fertilizers provide the fastest-acting nutrients. A disadvantage of synthetic fertilizers is that they wash out of the soil, especially in containers, and need to be applied more frequently. Also, they add no organic matter to improve soil texture and can burn plants if overused and allowed to build up in the soil.

The numbers on the fertilizer label give the percentages of nitrogen, phosphorus and potassium the fertilizer contains. Therefore,

5-10-5 means 20 percent active ingredients and 80 percent filler with the following active ingredients:

5 percent nitrogen (N): a leaf stimulant that promotes rapid growth and green color. Use on trees, shrubs, grass and leafy vegetables. Nitrogen is absorbed and recycled quickly by plants. Being highly soluble, nitrogen is easily washed from the soil by rain or irrigation and must be applied frequently.

10 percent phosphorus (P): stimulates flowering, promoting seed and fruit production. Use on blooming and fruiting plants. In arid regions, there is so much phosphorus in the soil that it causes salt problems. Phosphorus is highly insoluble, remaining in the soil for long periods, needing replenishment less frequently than nitrogen.

5 percent potassium (K): a root stimulant that promotes general well-being and winter hardiness. Use on all plants. Potassium is highly soluble but joins clay particles in the soil, so it is not quickly leached away and needs replenishing only once a year, usually in the spring, in good soils.

A complete fertilizer would be 5-10-5 or 10-10-10. An incomplete fertilizer would be 0-10-0 or 0-20-10. If you need a high-nitrogen fertilizer, look for one that has the first number higher that the other two; for a high-phosphorus fertilizer, look for one with the middle number the highest; for a high-potassium fertilizer, look for one with the third number the highest.

In addition to the primary nutrients (nitrogen, phosphorus and potassium), plants also need secondary nutrients (calcium, magnesium and sulfur). Secondary nutrients are present in most soils and do not need replenishing. In areas of high rainfall, however, calcium and magnesium are leached from the soil, and lime (calcium carbonate) should be added to lower acidity. In arid regions, calcium and magnesium dominate, and it may be necessary to add sulfur in the form of sulfate to make the soil less alkaline.

Micronutrients or trace elements (zinc, iron, magnesium, copper, boron, molybdenum, cobalt and chlorine) are needed for plant growth but in very small quantities. These should be added only if a soil test shows a deficiency.

Acidic fertilizers, which alter the chemical makeup of alkaline soils, are used to make iron available in a usable form.

How and When to Fertilize

Most nursery and container-grown stock does not require fertilizer at planting time or during the first year. When transplanting within your garden, fertilize after new growth begins. To determine what fertilizer you need to maintain established plants, or when transplanting, consult the following sections or ask your local garden center. Choose the right fertilizer for the job. Read labels carefully, and apply fertilizers according to the directions. Keep fertilizers away from the stems and leaves of plants and the trunks of trees. Never fertilize dry soil, and water thoroughly after applying fertilizer to settle granules and start nutrients toward the feeder roots. Do not fertilize trees, shrubs or herbaceous perennials after midsummer as you do not want to encourage leafy growth, which will not have time to harden before cold weather sets in.

Plants in nature grow without additional fertilizer except for fallen leaves and other decomposing natural matter. When a plant is expected to perform according to our directions, in places of our choice, at a rate we impose upon it, it may need an additional boost. Too much fertilizer, however, causes succulent weak growth at the expense of solid plant structure.

TREES

Mature. Use high-nitrogen tree spikes (10-5-5) or have an arborist deep-root feed the trees if they show signs of stress or poor leaf color.

Immature. Use high-nitrogen granular fertilizer (10-5-5) in early spring; broadcast, or spread, evenly beneath the drip line of the tree.

Fruit. Use high-nitrogen granular fertilizer (10-5-5) in early spring; broadcast evenly beneath the drip line of the tree. Feed again after flowering.

SHRUBS

Use high-phosphorus fertilizer (5-10-5) in early spring; spread evenly beneath the canopy of the plant. Feed again after flowering. Use an acid-based high-nitrogen fertilizer (5-10-5) on acid-loving plants.

LAWNS

Cool-season grasses (bent, fescue, Kentucky bluegrass, rye). Apply a high-nitrogen, slow-release fertilizer (20-1-10) in early spring and again in late fall. Heavily irrigated lawns may require more frequent treatment.

Warm-season grasses (bahia, Bermuda, centipede, St. Augustine, zoysia). Apply a balanced, slow-release fertilizer (10-10-10) in early spring and again in late fall, or more frequently on heavily irrigated lawns.

Apply lime in the fall if the pH reading is below 6.0 or 7.0.

When applying "weed-and-feed" products, use caution. Be sure to choose the correct product for your grass type and apply at the specified time. Be aware of the possible runoff of chemicals into the ground water supply or nearby ponds and streams.

GROUND COVERS

Sprinkle ground-cover beds with high-phosphorus granular fertilizer (5-10-5) or work in dehydrated manure in early spring.

PERENNIALS

Use high-phosphorus granular fertilizer (5-10-5) or aged or dehydrated manure in early spring sparingly in a ring around each plant as it emerges.

ANNUALS

Incorporate a high-phosphorus continuous-release fertilizer (5-10-5) into the soil at planting time and fertilize every three to four weeks during the growing season with a water-soluble, balanced fertilizer (10-10-10).

BULBS

Feed bulbs at planting time with bulb food or a balanced fertilizer (10-10-10) and again in the early spring or summer.

VEGETABLES

Use water-soluble foliar fertilizer or manure tea at transplanting time or when leafy vegetables show signs of poor leaf development. Fertilize established vegetables by side-dressing: spread an even row of high-phosphorus fertilizer (5-10-5) down each side of a row or encircle each plant. Work carefully into the soil and water thoroughly.

HERBS

Most herbs, if planted in moderately rich well-drained soil, do not need summer feeding. Instead, dig a small amount of compost into established beds each fall.

GRAPEVINES, BERRY BUSHES AND STRAWBERRIES

Use a balanced granular fertilizer (10-10-10) in a ring around each established plant in early spring or when planting. Feed again after harvesting.

Chapter 6

Lawn Care

Planting a lawn of grass requires the same attention to soil preparation as any other plant. Your choice of the seed or sod suitable for your lawn will be determined by your climate and the amount of sun available. There are grasses for both sunny and shady conditions. There are cool-season grasses, used in northern climates (bent, fescue, Kentucky bluegrass, rye) that grow actively in spring and summer, slowing down in summer months. Common in southern climates, there are warm-season grasses (bahia, Bermuda, centipede, St. Augustine, zoysia) that grow in the hot summer months and go dormant when the weather cools. Some warm-season grasses turn brown in the winter. In both northern and southern climates, grasses can be overseeded with winter rye to provide green lawns in winter. Research is underway to develop new grasses that will grow less high, need less frequent mowing, less fertilizer and less water.

Seeding a New Lawn

Clear the area of all vegetation including old sod, pebbles and other debris. If the area to be seeded is infested with weeds, water the site daily for a month to sprout dormant seeds, and eradicate them with a systemic herbicide or by shallow cultivation with a rake. Test the pH level of the soil. Rough grade the area sloping it slightly away from the house for drainage. Rake and cultivate to 6 inches. Enrich the soil with peat moss, compost, leaf mold and lime if recommended by the soil test. Level the area to be planted, lowering bumps and filling dips that will create future problems with drainage and mowing. Water the area the day before seeding. With a spreader, first sow half the seeds over the entire area, then sow the other half over the same area at right angles for complete coverage. Rake the seed in lightly. Apply a complete high-phosphorus lawn fertilizer. Mulch lightly with straw and roll the entire area to settle it. The mulch will decompose and disappear into the new lawn. Seeds can take from seven to forty-five days to germinate, depending upon the type of seed and weather conditions. Sprinkle the area daily until seeds sprout, then water thoroughly once or twice a week. Spring and early fall, when nighttime temperatures are cool, are the best times to start a lawn from cool-season seed. Warm-season grasses should be sown in late spring or early summer.

Overseeding an Established Lawn

Rake your lawn thoroughly to remove any build-up of debris, weeds and old grass (thatch) that has not decomposed. Fill in low spots with a mixture of topsoil and builder's sand. Level bumps and dips, rerake surface and reseed bare spots. Keep planted areas moist by light regular watering until the seed sprouts. For a green lawn in winter, overseed Bermuda grass or other grasses that tend to brown out with perennial rye grass.

Sodding a New Lawn

As an alternative to seeding, you may sod a lawn. Sod can be laid throughout the growing season. Sodding is more expensive than seeding, but it creates an instant lawn and works better than seed for slopes or other areas subject to erosion and wear. A sodded lawn will stand up to foot traffic more quickly than a seeded lawn. It takes about three weeks for sod to attach and begin to grow.

Sod is delivered on a pallet, rolled up or stacked. Keep it moist and shaded and lay it as soon as possible after delivery. Prepare a clean, weed-free, leveled dirt surface by raking just as you would for seeding. Shallow cultivation and herbicides will kill most annual and perennial seeds waiting to sprout. To allow for the thickness of the sod, lower the grade of the new lawn approximately $3/4$ inch. Then the

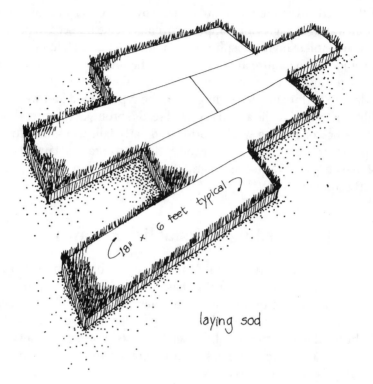

18" × 6 feet typical

laying sod

finished grade will be even with any adjoining paving or established planting beds. The day before installing the sod, water the soil to be covered. Lay the sod in straight strips on the soil surface. Using a straightedge, or a string line stretched between two stakes to establish direction, roll out the strips as carefully as possible. Do not stretch or bend the sod. Cut the sod with a serrated knife to fit curved edges. Make sure the edges of the strips are touching. For a smooth, even result, stagger the rolls of sod as if you were laying bands of bricks. When sodding a sloping area, lay the sod across the slope, starting at the bottom and working upward. Roll and water sod thoroughly upon installation and thereafter once or twice a week. Do not walk on a newly sodded lawn for three weeks. To test its readiness, gently lift a corner of the sod. If it resists, the roots have grown down into the soil below. If not, wait another week.

Maintaining a Healthy Lawn

A healthy lawn is the best defense against the invasion of weeds. Thick turf discourages weed seeds from germinating. Dig existing weeds out by hand or kill with repeated applications of selective systemic herbicides. If your soil is too acidic for good lawn grass, you can help neutralize the soil by spreading lime. Neutralizing will also rid the lawn of acid-loving weeds such as sheep sorrel. Lack of available nutrients encourages other weeds such as chickweed, sedge and speedwell.

For an attractive lawn, you must mow on a regular schedule and at the correct height for each type of grass. Weather conditions, the season of the year, soil fertility, moisture conditions and natural growth rate determine frequency of mowing, usually every five or seven days.

Mowing a lawn too short prevents the grass from developing deep roots. Allowing grass to become too tall between cuts may cause it to shade itself out. When cut, weakened stems may burn from exposure to strong sunlight making your lawn turn brown. Or the mower may simply knock over tall grass rather than cut it. If the lawn becomes too tall, mow several times, cutting shorter each time to gradually arrive at the correct height. If you mow often enough, it is not necessary to remove the clippings. Grass blades are essentially water and decompose rapidly. Leaving the clippings is a natural way to return organic material to the soil. An exception is a bent grass lawn from which most clippings should be removed.

A healthy lawn of creeping-type grasses, such as bent, can be cut very short, from $1/4$ inch to 1 inch. Kentucky bluegrass and fescue must be cut relatively high (2 to 3 inches). When you seed or sod your lawn, ask your supplier for the correct mowing height for your type of grass.

Grass should not be mowed when it is wet, as it will cut unevenly and the clippings will mat on the lawn and in the mower. To protect cool-season grasses from heat damage during hot dry spells in summer, mow less and raise mowing height to $3^1/2$ inches. Do not fertilize dry grass.

Watering, after proper mowing, is the second vital factor in maintaining your lawn. In moderate climates, your lawn, if it has not dried out and is in active growth, requires the equivalent of an inch of water a week. In periods of drought and high temperatures on sandy soil, it may need an additional 2 inches a week. Water may be supplied by rain, sprinklers or irrigation systems. To test the amount of water supplied by your sprinkling system, set several empty coffee cans at intervals across the lawn to find out how much they collect. For deep healthy roots, the water should penetrate the lawn to a depth of 4 to 6 inches. On heavy clay soils, a long, slow, deep soak is best. Apply the water only as fast as the soil can absorb it. On sandy soil, which drains rapidly, the equivalent amount of water should be delivered in several shorter applications.

The third factor for a healthy lawn is the regular application of lawn fertilizer for vigorous growth, resistance to disease and good color. Overfeeding, however, can lead to oversucculent growth and fungus diseases. Apply fertilizer only when the lawn is actively growing. Cool-season grasses grow more rapidly during spring and fall. They become dormant in the heat of summer. They should be fertilized in the early spring as growth begins and twice again in the fall. The fall applications will help the lawn thicken to repair any damage from summer heat and to prepare for winter. Feed warm-season grasses in mid- to late spring when they break dormancy; continue throughout the growing season.

Feed new lawns with a high-nitrogen (for growth), high-phosphorus (for root growth) fertilizer. After the lawn is established, continue with a high-nitrogen fertilizer. Potassium is also necessary for good growth but in smaller amounts. Include it in applications before seasons of stress—to cool-season grasses before summer heat begins and to warm-season grasses in the fall.

In areas of alkaline soil, if your lawn fails to grow or green up, even after watering in the correct amount of lawn fertilizer, you have chlorosis, or a lack of available iron in the soil. Test the soil and, if indicated, treat with a fertilizer containing iron.

Lawns that become compacted, crusted or waterlogged can be aerated. This is more likely to be necessary on clay or clay-loam soils although these same conditions can occur in sandy soils. Heavy foot traffic, constant mowing (especially in the same pattern) and surface runoff during heavy rains compound the problem. Aerating removes plugs of soil from the lawn, opening it up to permit more rapid penetration of air, water and fertilizer into the root zone, thus enhancing deep root growth. Aeration is generally done at the beginning of the growing season.

Dethatching removes accumulated grass stems and roots growing close to the surface. These accumulate on a compacted soil surface because of overwatering and overfertilizing.

There is nothing natural about a traditional lawn, but many Americans cannot imagine their neighborhoods without them. Like the front parlor used only for guests, the front lawn is something to admire, to labor over at great cost, but rarely to enjoy. Lawn grasses, like wild grasses, want to grow at least knee-high but are prevented from doing so by constant mowing. Because you remove the long blades that would collect and photosynthesize sunlight and nutrients the plant needs to feed itself, you must be willing to replace that nourishment with copious amounts of water and fertilizer. Water is in diminishing supply in some areas. Heavy applications of fertilizers and herbicides contaminate surface and underground water supplies.

Although grass is the best ground cover for heavily trafficked areas or as a play space for children, and is unequaled for setting off flower displays and shrub borders, every gardener should consider reducing the extent of mowed grass areas and using drought-tolerant varieties of grass.

Chapter 7

Garden Care

Maintaining your garden is a year-round affair. You can make it simpler by identifying and scheduling the various tasks involved. All gardens need pruning, fertilizing, lawn care, insect and disease control. These are discussed elsewhere. This chapter outlines the techniques and timing of other basic maintenance tasks: watering, weeding and mulching, staking, deadheading, harvesting flowers and herbs and seasonal garden cleanups.

Watering

Lack of water causes distress in plants and endangers their health, leaving them susceptible to insects and disease. You should water in new plants slowly and thoroughly to settle them into the ground, putting their roots in contact with the soil and forcing out any pockets of air. When you install large plants, water them in halfway through the procedure to settle the soil in the planting hole and again when the planting is completed. Water anytime the soil is dry below the surface or if plants look withered.

Water in the early morning or late afternoon. Watering at high noon may damage plants, as droplets that cling to the leaves can act as small lenses, focusing the sun's rays and actually burning the foliage. Also, watering in the heat of the day is wasteful: up to 50 percent of water from sprinklers can evaporate in the air or before it has had a chance to soak into the ground. If you water late in the day, avoid directing water onto the foliage itself; foliage that is continuously wet at night invites fungi, mold and mildew.

Always water plants thoroughly and deeply to encourage the roots, which seek out moisture, to grow downward. Light sprinkling develops shallow-rooted plants, which will suffer in periods of drought or extreme cold. Water under the entire leaf spread of the plant, soaking the root zone. Overwatering forces the oxygen out of the soil. Plants need oxygen, not only for general growth, but also to enable them to absorb water. So both overwatering and underwatering can result in a withered look.

Clay soil, which retains water and impedes its passage, requires deep, slow watering, but avoid overwatering in areas with "caliche" soil or hardpan, a cement-like, impervious layer of calcium carbonate below the soil surface. Sandy soil, which drains quickly, requires more frequent watering. Wind and high temperatures dry out plants and soil more rapidly, so extra watering will be needed under those conditions.

Plants have different moisture requirements at different stages of development.

- Seeds need constant moisture to germinate. Sprinkle soil once or twice a day.
- Seedlings and transplants, which have shallow roots, need frequent light watering.
- Shrubs and trees, which are deep-rooted plants, grow best with deep but less frequent watering.
- Newly planted or transplanted stock is especially vulnerable until it is thoroughly established (as long as three to five years for major trees and shrubs).
- Newly seeded lawns should be sprinkled daily until seeds sprout, then twice a week until the lawn is established at mowing height. Once a lawn is established, water it heavily in order to encourage deep roots, then water again only when surface is dry.

During periods of below normal rainfall and high temperatures, plants will show drought stress (withered or burned foliage, leaf drop, color change, drooping branches).

During a severe water shortage you should establish priorities: water trees, shrubs and lawns, respectively. The lawn may brown out but will come back if it is well established. It is sad to lose annuals, but they can be replaced next season. Pay special attention to newly installed plants, which are at most risk. These plants should be watered twice or more each week. If a drenching rain falls and the soil immediately surrounding the plant seems moist, forego the second watering that week. To deep-water a parched tree, position a hose at the base of the tree near the drip line and let it run slowly for several hours. Move it around the tree several times. (You are trying to get the water deep down into the soil.)

Try to maintain a steady moisture level during the growing season in spring to encourage flowering and fruiting, and during summer to reduce plant stress caused by heat and drought.

In cold climates, taper off watering in the fall to allow woody growth to harden and dormancy to set in before frost and freezing weather.

In warmer climates, or in areas lacking snow coverage or adequate winter rains, continue some watering during winter. Roots continue to grow even though the top of the plant is dormant. Plants exposed to desiccating winds are especially vulnerable.

To simplify watering, group plants in zones according to their watering needs. Plant the most demanding near the house. Moving away from the house, plant the transitional group next, then the self-sustaining ones on the edges of your property.

To conserve water, form earthen saucers around larger plants and apply mulch when planting.

Some hand watering will be necessary in most gardens. Many gardeners find it a soothing task, but hand watering is time consuming, requiring great patience, and it is not practical in large gardens. There are other options.

Portable sprinklers include impulse- or impact-type sprinklers, revolving sprinklers, fixed sprinklers designed to shoot water through holes in specified patterns (changeable by turning a dial), oscillating sprinklers, which shoot water long distances high in the air, and traveling types with revolving heads that move across the lawn. These sprinklers deliver differing volumes of water in different patterns over varying distances. Most can be regulated for output and distance.

Choose a type that fits your garden. Portable sprinklers need no installation, only a hose attachment. They can be moved about the garden and placed as needed. They are useful for lawns and ground-cover plantings, but the spray can damage delicate perennials, annuals and vegetables. Place empty coffee cans around the area being sprinkled to see how much water accumulates. Plants, including the lawn, need the equivalent of an inch of water a week—more in hot, dry weather.

Soaker hoses—wound carefully through planting beds, laid at the base of a hedge or cut and attached at intervals to a main supply line and laid in parallel rows in the vegetable or cutting garden—will deliver water slowly, steadily and deeply through thousands of tiny pores over a 6-inch to 1-foot swath depending on the length of time water is delivered and the type of soil. Soaker hoses can be covered with mulch (which will absorb some water) or buried in the soil to protect them from sunlight and to keep them out of sight. They can be moved about as watering needs change. They are sometimes used with automated irrigation systems.

Automatic irrigation systems include timer-activated pop-up and fixed sprinkler heads. The heads are attached to an underground piping layout. Systems can be controlled manually or automatically with a clock timer. They are useful for large areas of garden or lawn.

Drip irrigation systems apply water directly onto the soil through a system of emitters set along a hose or pipe buried in the ground. They can be automatic or manual. They make the most economical use of water, applying it to the ground, reducing loss of water through evaporation and keeping moisture off foliage. Emitters can be balanced to deliver from $1/2$ to 5 gallons an hour as fine mist or as a light sprinkle. They are excellent for slopes where runoff might cause erosion, for vegetable gardens and other complex plantings. They can be installed to water plants growing in containers.

Because plants have ever-changing moisture requirements as seasons and weather conditions change, automatic watering systems should be reviewed every month. More plants survive moderate drought situations better than overly wet conditions.

Weeding

Weeds have been described as plants found in the wrong places. They range from chickweed and nutsedge to wild chrysanthemum and bittersweet vine. They can arrive by being blown by the wind, as seeds dropped by birds, as "hitchhikers" with plants from the garden center and nursery or in topsoil and organic mulches. Their seeds can lie dormant in the soil for years, waiting for an opportunity to sprout. There are annual (chickweed, ragweed) and perennial (bindweed, Canadian thistle) weeds, weeds that have long taproots (dandelion, plantain) and weeds that spread by runners (yarrow, creeping buttercup). Some weeds continue flowering and setting seed after they have been yanked from the ground; some reroot easily, so be careful where you toss them. All weeds compete with garden plants for valuable space and nutrients.

There are two major weed crops a year, in spring and fall. You should remove the first during spring cleanup before new growth begins. You should remove the second during fall cleanup. Act promptly to get rid of all weeds when they are small, before they become entangled in perennials and shrubs, invade the lawn, climb the trees and before they set seed and multiply. It's easier to weed after a rain or thorough watering, especially when pulling weeds by hand. You want to get the roots, not just the leafy tops. Avoid disturbing shallow-rooted plants (most annuals, perennials and vegetables) while weeding. Snip out unwanted seedlings with scissors to avoid uprooting adjacent plants or exposing latent weed seeds. Most woody plants will tolerate rougher treatment, including light cultivation with a hoe in the planting bed. Weeds with shallow root systems can be hand weeded or removed by light cultivation. Small patches can be smothered with mulches, boards, heavy layers of newspapers or black plastic if these covers exclude all light and air and are left in place for several weeks. Remove weeds with long taproots (long, central, vertical roots) by cutting under the soil surface with an old kitchen knife or an asparagus knife to remove the entire root. Use a garden fork to remove large infestations of shallow-rooted weeds that spread by runners. Some weeds will resist all attempts made by hand to eliminate them and will require treatment with a systemic weed killer.

Pre-emergent weed killers prevent weed seeds from germinating. They are applied as granules or spray to lawns and bare soil in vegetable gardens and shrub and flower beds where nonharmful to existing plant material. They prevent growth of seedlings for three to six weeks. As these weed killers indiscriminately prevent all seeds from germinating, do not sow grass or other seeds in the area for six weeks after applying.

You can buy organic and chemical weed killers (herbicides) formulated to eliminate weeds that are difficult to control by the above methods. Such weeds include Canadian thistle, goutweed, poison ivy and crabgrass. Systemic weed-killer sprays are absorbed by the stems and foliage of plants and transferred into the root systems. The effects of application may not show up for several weeks, but treated plants will eventually turn brown and die. Any portion of the liquid falling on the soil becomes inactive immediately, causing no lasting harm. Systemic sprays work best when the plants are in active growth.

Use herbicides with care, following the directions on the package. Mix as stated as there is no advantage to strengthening solutions. Remember that chemicals that kill weeds will also kill most garden plants. Labels will list especially sensitive plants. Be careful of drift on windy days and when using herbicides near shrub and tree roots and ponds and streams. (Chemicals spread quickly in water, interfering with aquatic ecosystems and surrounding vegetation.)

Mulching

Mulch is any material applied to soil to moderate or increase temperature, conserve moisture, suppress weeds or curtail compaction and erosion. Mulch can also look attractive, improving the appearance of your garden. Choose a mulch that is compatible in color and in scale with the texture and size of your planting. Mulch can be organic (shredded bark, pine needles, salt hay, straw, wood chips, cocoa shells). Some organic mulches amend the soil's chemistry (pine needles and oak leaves acidify soil); others increase friability and fertility (decomposing mulches add humus and organic matter). Inorganic mulches—pebbles or crushed stone—conserve moisture, make plantings appear more formal, aid drainage and last a long time.

In your vegetable garden, plastic mulches are particularly useful in controlling both moisture loss and weeds, but they are unsightly. They collect water in stagnant pools unless you puncture them at random intervals. Also, they do not decompose to add organic material to the soil. Use clear plastic to warm up the soil in spring but remove it before planting. Use black plastic under tomatoes, squash, melons and strawberries to prevent mud splash. Use geotextiles or landscape fabrics under a layer of gravel or shredded bark in service areas. This will help prevent weeds while permitting drainage.

Apply mulch 3 to 4 inches deep, leaving a space of several inches between the mulch and the base of any plants. Overmulching can lead to saturated soil conditions which force out oxygen necessary for growth. Piling mulch around tree trunks reduces air circulation and promotes decay and plant diseases. Plant roots tend to grow up into thick mulch, and they may dry out or freeze in the winter.

Mulch in late spring to conserve moisture after the soil has absorbed water from melting snow and spring rains. Mulch newly installed plants after watering in. If the soil is excessively dry, water thoroughly before you mulch.

Mulch in summer to reduce watering and soil crusting, to discourage weeds and to lower soil temperatures in the root zone.

Mulch in winter to prevent thawing and freezing of the ground and subsequent heaving of small and newly installed plants, and to prevent moisture loss and freeze damage to roots of tender plants. If there are mice, voles or moles nearby, wait until the ground has frozen before you mulch; otherwise, these animals may nest in the mulch and feast on your plants during the winter. Apply winter mulches 4 inches to 8 inches deep.

Light mulches like shredded pine bark nuggets, pine needles, leafy compost, boughs from discarded Christmas trees, salt hay and straw are good winter mulches because they don't pack down. Leaves (unless shredded) and grass clippings tend to hold too much moisture and make the soil soggy. Remove winter mulches gradually as the soil warms up in the spring.

When choosing a mulch, remember that dried pine needles, straw and evergreen boughs can be fire hazards in summer and winter.

Staking

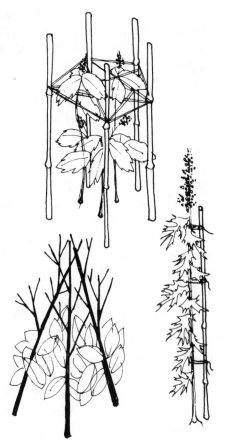

Some multistemmed plants need staking to prevent them from falling and crushing weaker plants, to keep the blooms at an angle where they can be enjoyed or to prevent them from toppling in wind and rain. Plants with heavy foliage and blooms will need 18-inch to 24-inch bamboo or metal stakes. These should be set in a circle of five or more surrounding the plant and pushed firmly into the ground. Loop garden twine around each stake and crisscross to opposite stakes, forcing a star shape within a wheel. The stems will grow up through the wheel, hiding the stakes and twine. Airy plants can be supported with small twiggy branches pruned from trees and shrubs. Set the branches in the ground, bending them inward around the plant as it emerges from the soil. Timing is important. You want to avoid a landscape of naked stakes, yet you must anticipate the blooming times when the plants will get out of control.

When staking a tall single-stemmed plant (delphinium, lilies) choose a stake that will be slightly shorter than the flowering stem when in bloom. Set it firmly in the ground, avoiding plant roots. First, tie soft twine or strips of old cloth securely to the stake, then encircle and tie the stem loosely so you do not choke it. Continue to tie the stem higher upon its stake as the plant grows.

Deadheading and Shearing Back

Deadheading means removing the spent blossoms from a plant to prevent the formation of seedpods and directing the energy of the plant into growth. Deadheading improves the appearance of shrubs (crape myrtle, lilac, rhododendron). With annuals, regular deadheading prolongs continuous bloom, and with perennials, rebloom.

Deadheading bulbs prevents the seed formation that saps the strength of the bulb for the following year. Leave bulb foliage to wither and turn yellow for a minimum of six weeks before removing it.

Some perennials (astilbe, coneflower, ornamental grasses, some sedums) need not be deadheaded and can be left to go to seed since their decorative seedpods are desirable additions to the garden, especially in winter. They also provide seed for the birds.

Shearing, or cutting back, annuals and perennials is more drastic than deadheading as it removes ragged stems and leaves to tidy and re-shape the plant after bloom. Some early summer-blooming perennials (salvia, evening primrose, veronica, geranium) can be severely cut back, resulting in a flush of fresh foliage. Some rebloom may occur.

Harvesting Flowers for Drying

Gather flowers before they are in full bloom, in the early morning after the dew has dried. For variety, gather blooms at different stages of maturity. Collect only undamaged specimens of different shapes, sizes, colors and textures. Strip off lower leaves; bind smaller flowers in bunches with a rubber band since stems will shrink; hang bunches upside down in a warm, dark, dry and well-ventilated spot. Larger flowers should hang separately. Plumes, such as astilbe, goldenrod and heather, may be dried upright in bottles or vases. Delicate flowers maintain their shape better if dried flat. Flowers are dry when their stems, particularly near the blossom, feel dry and crisp. This may take three to five weeks. To protect colors, store in a dark spot until ready to use.

Harvesting Herbs for Drying and Freezing

Cut herbs for potpourri and decorative use when they are in flower. Groom stems well, wash and dry on screens or tie in small bunches and hang in a dry, warm, airy spot. For the kitchen, cut herbs just before they go into flower. Hang to dry, strip and store in individual plastic bags or jars: marjoram, mint, oregano, rosemary, sage and thyme. Pat dry and freeze on the stem: basil, dill, parsley and tarragon. Chop and freeze chives. Store each kind of herb in a separate container.

Seasonal Care

Spring Cleanup

✿ Gradually remove winter mulches from bulb, perennial and shrub beds and add to compost pile.

✿ Remove protective winter screening from tender plants.

✿ Rake winter debris, leaves and twigs from lawns and planting beds. Add to compost pile.

✿ Cut back remaining ornamental grass or perennial stalks before new growth begins.

✿ Weed and edge beds.

✿ Rake and prepare annual beds. Lay out new beds for planting.

✿ Prepare vegetable beds.

✿ Check espaliers and climbers for loose ties.

✿ Clean greenhouses; sterilize pots and flats used for seedlings.

✿ Open and ventilate cold frames when temperature is above 40°F.

✿ Service irrigation systems, hoses and outdoor faucets (bibbs).

✿ Inventory supplies; clean, sharpen and oil tools, lawn mowers, spray equipment.

Fall Cleanup

🍁 Continue mowing and watering new grass. Lawn should be short as winter begins. Rake lawn regularly or leaves will mat and smother grass.

🍁 Add a layer of lime or lawn fertilizer to compost leaves to hasten decomposition. Keep moist.

🍁 Recycle shredded leaves as winter mulch on tender plants. Recycle oak leaves as mulch on acid-loving plants (rhododendrons, azaleas, hollies, etc.).

🍁 Dispose of foliage and fallen twigs of camellias, dogwood, gladiola, iris, peonies, roses and any other plants showing signs of disease.

🍁 Clean up perennial beds. Remove fallen leaves and other debris. Remove stakes and store for reuse. Cut perennial stalks back to 4 to 6 inches so you can find plants when spring comes.

🍁 Mark late-emerging perennials to avoid damaging them during spring cleanup.

🍁 Leave ornamental grasses, seed heads and dried fronds for winter interest.

🍁 In northern climates, lift tender summer bulbs, including tuberous begonia, caladium, canna, dahlia, gladiolus, and tritoma, after the first frost. Store in a cool cellar.

🍁 Remove spent annuals and compost.

🍁 Weed, shape and edge beds.

🍁 Update records of planting and harvesting dates. List gaps in planting, favorite varieties, quantities and qualities of harvest. Make a crop-rotation plan for next year.

🍁 Prepare soil in flower and vegetable beds for spring planting. Sow a green crop in vegetable beds to be turned under in the spring.

🍁 In cold climates, ventilate cold frames (see next section, "Adjuncts to Good Gardening") until ground has frozen; afterwards close and mulch lightly or cover with straw matting.

🍁 Prune and fasten climbers against wind damage.

🍁 Continue to feed fish in ponds until water freezes.

❀ Turn off water, drain hoses, service irrigation systems.

❀ Clean, sharpen and oil tools. Store any remaining liquid fertilizers, herbicides, insecticides in a safe frost-proof spot.

Winter Plant Protection

❊ Before ground freezes, if autumn has been dry, thoroughly water shallow-rooted plants (i.e., dogwood), broadleaf evergreens, newly planted trees and newly planted bulb beds.

❊ Water newly planted and established broadleaf and needle evergreens during a midwinter thaw or a dry winter season. Roots continue to grow underground when temperatures are above freezing and need a continual supply of moisture.

❊ Spray broadleaf evergreens and newly planted needle evergreens with antidesiccant (available from garden supply stores) to prevent foliage dehydration when temperature is above 40°F. Repeat during midwinter.

❊ Move tender (half-hardy) container plants into the greenhouse or cold frame. In warmer regions, sink containers into the ground to protect root ball during cold snaps.

❊ Cover marginally hardy plants with burlap, leaves or baskets if a freeze is predicted. Remove the coverings as the temperature rises.

❊ In cold areas, mound up 10 to 12 inches of extra soil or leaves around roses to protect from winter damage.

❊ After the ground freezes, mulch bulb beds, perennials and other small plants to prevent heaving of plants during periods of thawing and freezing.

❊ To protect boxwood and other brittle shrubs from heavy snowfall, encircle plant with twine, drawing it through and interweaving it several times within the branches of the shrub, or install covers. Tie ropes around columnar plants at several heights to prevent snow damage.

❊ Check guy wires on newly planted trees; tighten if heaved by frost.

❊ Check trees and shrubs for rodent damage; protect by wrapping with wire mesh or tree wrap. Wrap must reach higher than maximum snowfall.

✳ Shake or sweep snow from evergreens; let icy coverings on branches melt naturally.

✳ Use sand or ashes on icy walks and drives (salt damages plants and lawns).

✳ To prevent bare spots on next spring's lawn, avoid walking on frozen grass.

Adjuncts to Good Gardening

Managing Garden Waste/ Recycling Garden Debris

Until recently, grass clippings and leaves accounted for 10 to 25 percent of all waste sent to landfills annually. Many states will no longer accept grass clippings or other garden waste in landfills. Therefore, all gardeners must find ways to recycle such materials back into the garden in the form of compost or mulch. By carefully salvaging and recycling all healthy garden debris, including grass clippings, fallen leaves, evergreen needles, light clippings, old flower and vegetable plants and some kitchen refuse, you can produce your own valuable organic material to benefit your garden. As shredding hastens decomposition, much of this material, especially leaves, can be reduced for composting by running over it with a rotary mower. Heavier materials will require a mechanical chipper or shredder but will produce a continual supply of compost or mulch. Never compost diseased plants, plants suffering from severe insect infestations, grass clippings treated with chemical insecticides and weed killers or sawdust from treated wood, which may present a health hazard.

Lawn clippings. Grass clippings account for 75 percent of total yard waste. New recycling or mulching mowers are designed to shred clippings more finely. Mowing more often, every five to six days, and using slow-release lawn fertilizer will allow you to return grass clippings to the lawn immediately.

Making and using compost. Compost is a natural, organic fertilizer and soil conditioner, invaluable in all areas of the garden. Recycling garden debris to make your own compost will reduce your fertilizer bills. Compost is safe to use and will not burn your plants. It can be tilled into your garden as humus and fertilizer, used as a soil conditioner for clay or sandy soils, to side-dress plants and vegetables, to topdress the lawn when reseeding and as potting soil. It can be used as mulch to help control weeds and retain moisture.

Compost can be collected in a pile or stored more neatly in a bin or a series of bins. You can buy or make the bin. It can be round or square, made of a circle of heavy wire, cement blocks, boards, bricks or other building materials except treated wood. It can be three-sided, allowing you to push the wheelbarrow in for easy dumping, running it up a board as the pile rises.

compost bins

Choose a level semishady location protected from heavy rainfall. A minimum of 3 cubic feet is required to produce the necessary heat (160° F) and hold it long enough to do the job. The pile should be at least 3 feet across, not more than 4 feet high and as long as you wish. Piled higher, it will compress under its own weight, forcing out the air necessary for decomposition. It must be ventilated at the sides and open to the earth at the bottom to allow microorganisms and earthworms from the ground to interact with the compost and excess water to drain away. Side-by-side bins allow one to ripen while you collect new wastes in the other.

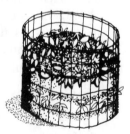

Shred the materials to be composted into small pieces with a chipper to make as much surface as possible for decomposing. Strike a balance between wet, high-nitrogen, usually green materials—sod, farm-animal manure, kitchen wastes—and dry, carbon-rich, brown materials—leaves and other dried plant matter, shredded newspaper, sawdust, straw. Layer wet and dry ingredients. If the compost is lacking green materials, add a few handfuls of high-nitrogen fertilizer. If it's lacking manure, sprinkle some garden soil or aged compost on each layer; this will provide necessary microorganisms. Keep the compost moist by spraying it with the garden hose, but do not saturate the pile because this drives out the air necessary for composting action. Grass clippings should be mixed with dry leaves to prevent them from matting.

After a year or longer, compost materials will decompose by themselves, but the process can be speeded up by layering the ingredients, keeping them moist and turning the pile. As the decomposing materials begin to break down (in a couple of weeks), the heat will rise in the pile. As the pile begins to cool down, it will shrink and become compact. Turn it to introduce more oxygen and continue the decomposing. The compost is ready when the temperature cools. Turn the pile at this point, sifting it if you wish, adding any outsized pieces to begin the next pile. To store finished compost, cover it to keep rain from leaching out the nutrients.

Kitchen and other household wastes suitable for the compost pile include fruit and vegetable trimmings, peels, rinds, seeds, bread, coffee grounds, unbleached coffee filters, tea leaves, eggshells, wood ash and small wood chips.

Not suitable are any fatty food waste, bone, chicken parts, fish scraps, dairy products, eggs, lard, meat, peanut butter, salad dressing, vegetable oil or household pet manure. These will produce odors and attract flies, raccoons, rodents and other pests (and pet manures may carry diseases).

A properly constructed compost pile will pasteurize the contents, killing weeds, seeds, insect eggs and many disease-causing organisms. Using the right materials, sufficient moisture and occasionally turning the compost pile to expose new material to the air prevent bad odors from forming.

Cold Frames

Build or install a cold frame to prolong the growing season. A cold frame is a protective box with a transparent top that provides warmth and protection for tender plants. Usually without a bottom, it sits directly on the ground and can be used as a seedbed or as a base for planting trays or potted plants. It collects heat from the sun during the day and retains it during the night, preventing damage from low nighttime temperatures and cold winds. The sides can be made of wood, railroad ties, masonry or straw bales. The top can be of glass, fiberglass or plastic sheeting. The top should open easily on hinges (or be removable) for ventilation to prevent heat and moisture build-up. A hinged top can be held open by adjustable props.

Place the cold frame in full sun with an eastern or southern exposure, against a wall, if possible, for additional heat accumulation, and protected from snowdrifts and wind. A heavy tarp or rug can be placed over the top for extra insulation at night in winter.

Install a thermometer and check interior temperature on a regular basis. A convenient size is 3 feet wide by 6 feet long, so you can reach across from front to back, and 18 inches high in back and 12 inches in front. The cold frame top is usually slanted to catch as much winter sun as possible and drain snow and rain runoff away from the structure.

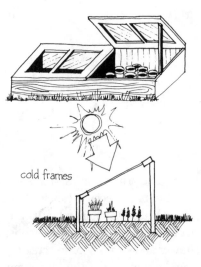

cold frames

In warm climates, the top and sides of a cold frame can be simply made with translucent plastic sheeting stapled onto a wooden frame. Lightweight portable versions of this frame are useful to move about the garden in any climate to provide temporary shelter for tender plants.

Modern cold frames, which can be ordered by mail from nursery or greenhouse supply companies, are designed with vents or lids that open automatically as soon as the temperature reaches 75° F. (This is something to consider if you are not home when the temperature fluctuates.)

Use the cold frame for sprouting annuals, perennials and vegetables for the spring and summer garden, for hardening off seedlings started indoors, before setting garden center and mail-order plants out in the garden, for divisions and cuttings taken in summer, for sowing late fall or winter crops, for overwintering tender perennials and potted herbs and for forcing early spring bulbs for the house.

During the winter, plants in cold frames rarely need watering, but check spring seedlings and summer cuttings frequently. If you plan to use the cold frame to house potted plants only, cover the ground with several inches of gravel for drainage.

Chapter 8

Growing Herbs, Vegetables and Fruits

The prime interest of many gardeners lies in growing things to eat. For them, a special area should be set aside for a full-scale kitchen garden. Other gardeners who want to grow just a few herbs, perhaps some fruits and vegetables, should consider incorporating them in ornamental flower and shrub borders, creating a sort of "edible landscape," or planting them in a collection of containers on the patio or balcony.

Mixing Herbs, Vegetables and Fruits in the Garden

Several well-known herbs, thyme, lavender and rosemary, are at home anywhere in the garden, at any time of the year. They make charming and fragrant patio plants, especially when planted in combination with flowering annuals. Like many herbs, they tolerate hot sun and dry soil. In cold climates, rosemary can be moved indoors to winter as a houseplant. Train it on a frame as an ornamental topiary.

Parsley, colorful lettuces and alpine strawberries make useful edges for planting beds in front of flowering shrubs or tall perennials. Use rhubarb as a focal point in the garden, dill and bronze fennel for contrasting color and feathery texture. In late summer, when gardens take on an exhausted look, decorative peppers, eggplants and okra are just beginning to mature and can take the place of annuals and perennials. Globe artichokes, with their stunning foliage and purple thistle flowers and the coarse texture of kale, mingle well with ornamental grasses. The fronds of maturing asparagus add golden tones to autumn gardens.

Use lowbush blueberries as a ground cover. They ripen in the same acidic soil preferred by rhododendrons and azaleas. In autumn, the foliage turns deep red. Fruit trees offer beautiful spring bloom, summer shade and colorful fruit. Dwarf varieties can be grown in tubs to enhance the patio or add interest to an herb or vegetable garden. Grape and kiwi vines are both decorative and edible candidates for trellises and arbors.

The Separate Vegetable Garden

The ideal location for a separate vegetable garden is a sunny, south-facing site, gently sloping if possible, airy but protected from strong winds. Light is the most important factor as vegetables require 6 to 8 hours of direct sunlight a day and warm temperatures, 60° F and above. Leafy crops, lettuce, spinach, parsley and chervil, do reasonably well in partial shade. Carrots and beets need more light but will produce with morning sun. Stay away from greedy tree and shrub roots (beyond the drip line or outer foliage reach of trees and shrubs), which sap nutrients and moisture, and stay away from large trees that cast shadows. The existing soil, if poor and rocky, can be improved over the years with sufficient additions of manure, leaf mold and compost, and with the pH level adjusted to slightly acidic (6.1 to 6.8), which suits most popular vegetables. Hedges and fences can reduce exposure to wind. A hose bibb, cistern or rain barrel can supply water and should be conveniently located nearby.

You will need a fence if visiting rabbits and raccoons are problems. For deer, which are becoming a major problem in woodland areas that are being urbanized, it takes an 8 to 10 foot fence, electrified, for complete protection, not something the average gardener can manage, financially or physically. Lightweight floating row covers draped over low-growing crops and repellent scent sprays are worth trying on vulnerable crops.

If birds are a problem, use netting to protect ripening fruit on trees and large shrubs. In some areas, it may be necessary to erect chicken-wire cages, high enough to walk around in, to save fruits from hungry birds.

Preparing the site. The site for the vegetable garden can be roughly prepared in late fall. Add necessary amendments which will settle and work their way into the soil over winter. Add manure and rotted compost to heavy or sandy soil. A green cover crop (winter rye, buckwheat) can be sown in the fall after the last harvest to be turned under to enrich the soil before spring planting. Come spring, do not work wet soil as`it ruins the structure. Wait until it dries sufficiently so that a handful of clenched dirt will crumble easily when dropped. The garden should be cultivated to a depth of 8 to 12 inches; rocks, weeds and other debris should be removed. Break up large clumps of dirt. Add fertilizer just prior to planting. The soil should be friable, of even texture and yield easily to your garden tools. Rake evenly. Do not overwork soil, which is easy to do with a rototiller. Fine, powdery soil dries out too quickly.

In areas with late springs or drainage problems, plant in beds where the soil is raised up by grading or supported by treated lumber or railroad ties. The soil in these limited spaces will be easy to improve and maintain. In raised beds, it will warm up faster and drain well. In high summer, however, raised beds may need additional watering. Contrarily, in arid regions, beds can be sunk to collect as much moisture as possible.

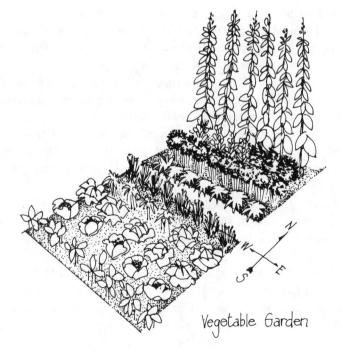

Vegetable Garden

Laying out the garden. In a large vegetable garden, plan 18-inch-wide paths between rows and mulch them. Planting beds that are no wider than 3 or 4 feet can be cultivated from both sides and need not be walked on, eliminating a major cause of soil compaction. If possible, the rows should run east to west to maximize sunlight, but on any steep slope rows should go across the grade.

You can plant in single or double rows or in 4-foot blocks. Single rows require many paths but can be cultivated with power tools. Use for cucumbers, corn, peas, melons, okra, potatoes, squash and tomatoes.

Wide, or double rows, are adaptable to salad crops, root crops and herbs. They reduce the amount of planting space taken up by walkways. Clustered plants reduce weeds and soil compaction, conserving moisture. Rows are easily harvested.

Planting blocks or squares are reachable from all four sides and lend themselves to many small crops.

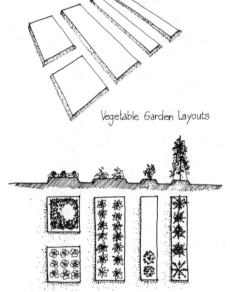

Vegetable Garden Layouts

Place taller crops and those grown on poles and trellises north of other crops so they will not shade out lower-growing ones. In high summer, however, that shade may allow you to grow cool-season crops such as salad greens. Or, gain shade and cooler temperatures from trellises or shade cloth.

Maximizing space and production. Prepare the garden in the fall for early spring planting of peas; cover that portion of the bed with black plastic. Tack it down with stones or logs. In early spring, remove the plastic, give the soil a light raking and plant.

Start vegetables and herbs indoors in early spring in the cold frame or in nursery beds in summer for fall planting to quickly fill empty spots. You will gain six to eight weeks of growing time.

Protect seedlings from late spring or early fall frosts with light-weight polyester fabric covers or "hot caps" and from hot sun with shade netting. Mulch carrots for winter harvest, parsnips for spring harvest.

Plant fast-maturing vegetables (lettuce, mustard greens, radishes, spinach) between slow-maturing ones (eggplant, peppers, tomatoes). They will be harvested before the slow developers need the room. Try radishes in rows of carrots or parsley, early lettuce between broccoli seedlings or tomato plants.

Lengthen the harvesting period by sowing short rows of the same vegetables at weekly intervals but in different areas. Follow leafy, or top, crops with a root vegetable.

As you harvest one crop, plant another. For example, beets, carrots or broccoli follow peas. Peppers follow spring lettuce. Fall spinach and a fall crop of carrots or beets complete the succession.

Create extra space by planting in containers: vegetables with modest root systems will be the most successful (carrots, eggplant, lettuce, onions, peppers, dwarf varieties of tomatoes). Try dwarf hybrid cucumbers and tomatoes.

Herbs flourish in containers. Rampant ones, like mint, can be kept under control. Many are tolerant of dry conditions. Plants in containers will require more attention than those growing in the ground. Choose the largest containers possible and protect them from wind and rain.

Choosing the crops. When deciding what to grow, especially if you have limited space, choose vegetables that are not easily available commercially in your area or that are not obtainable in good quality or in the varieties you prefer. Choose tried-and-true hybrid varieties for extra vigor and yield and those listed as "disease resistant." Be sure to choose varieties that will mature during your growing season (frost-free days in your zone). There are many companies that offer seeds for special crops, for heirloom varieties, baby vegetables, ethnic cooking and unusual culinary herbs.

Planting. Information on seed packets will give planting dates, germination times, the number of days to harvest and other pertinent information. As weather conditions vary from year to year, planting and harvesting dates are never absolute. Lengthen your growing season by starting crops in flats or peat pots indoors and transplanting them out when the soil warms up. (See Chapter 12.)

Plant perennial vegetables and herbs, which are sold as seedlings in small pots or market packs, as you would plant any other perennial, giving them a permanent place in the garden. Treat annual vegetables and herbs as you would any other annual, starting them from seeds, which are sold in packets, or as seedlings sold in market packs. Soil preparation, starting seeds, general planting techniques and planting in containers are fully discussed in other chapters.

Use a line stretched between two stakes as a guide when planting long rows. Use the back of a rake to mark furrows.

When to plant. Plant perennial vegetables as soon as they become available at your garden center or from mail-order sources.

- Perennial vegetables: artichokes (seeds, plants), asparagus (crowns), chayote (a vine, or plant the gourd-shaped fruit), horseradish (root sections), rhubarb (roots or crowns).
- Perennial herbs: burnet, chives, French tarragon, lavender, lemon balm, mint, oregano, rosemary, sage, sorrel, sweet marjoram (tender), thyme, winter savory.

Timing for sowing or setting out annual vegetables and herbs differs and depends on the first and last frost-free dates in your zone (your growing season) and the temperature of the soil. Use a soil thermometer to check soil temperatures. Early spring crops like lettuce, spinach and peas will germinate in soil as cold as 40° F, although if the soil is too wet, the seeds will rot. Tomatoes and peppers require 60° F or higher. Cucumbers, some melons, okra, pumpkins and squash germinate best with soil temperatures between 60° and 80° F. Few can stand temperatures over 90° F, with exceptions such as corn, cucumbers, melons, okra and turnips.

Annual herbs and vegetables are grouped into two categories: cool season and warm season. Beyond that, they can be divided into cool-season hardy, cool-season half-hardy, warm-season tender, and warm-season very tender. Begin in the spring with cool-season crops, and as the soil warms, add less-hardy crops. Approaching fall as the nights and soil cool, you can plant spring- or cool-season crops again, but allow enough time for them to mature before the first frost.

- Annual vegetables:
  Cool-season hardy: broccoli, Brussels sprouts, cabbage, collards, garlic, kale, kohlrabi, leeks, lettuce and other salad greens, onions, peas (edible pod and garden), radishes, spinach, turnips.
  Cool-season half-hardy: beets, carrots, cauliflower, celery, Chinese cabbage, endive, mustard, parsnips, potatoes, rutabagas, salsify, Swiss chard.
  Warm-season tender: cowpeas, New Zealand spinach, pole beans, snap beans, soybeans, sweet corn.
  Warm-season very tender: cucumber, eggplant, lima beans, muskmelon, okra, peppers, pumpkin, squash, sweet potatoes, tomatoes, watermelon.

- Annual herbs:
  Cool-season hardy: parsley (Treat parsley, which is a biennial, as an annual).
  Warm-season tender: chervil, coriander, cumin, dill.
  Warm-season very tender: basil.

Maintaining the vegetable garden. Keep a neat, clean, well-weeded, mulched and watered garden, and treat pest problems promptly to insure a good harvest.

General information regarding watering, weeding, mulching and staking can be found in Chapter 7. The following are additional instructions pertaining to growing vegetables.

Thin emerging crops according to directions on seed packets for proper spacing. Use thinnings as greens in salads. Leaf lettuce can be sheared rather than pulled. New leaves will appear. Harvest vegetables when they are young and tender. Before they rot, pull and add overgrown ones to the compost. Continual harvesting encourages production. Train vining plants on poles, trellises or netting.

Watering. Drip irrigation is the most effective method for watering vegetables, especially in a large garden. In general, vegetables need a steady supply of water delivered to their root zones for continuous growth to develop size and flavor, although there are periods of special need. Germinating seeds need careful light watering to keep the soil surface moist while not dislodging the seeds. Transplants should be watered frequently during the first two weeks after being set out until they become established. Leafy crops—salad greens, including spinach—are shallow-rooted and need a steady supply. Root crops—beets, carrots, potatoes, turnips—will stop growing during hot spells if not given sufficient water, becoming pithy or fibrous. Cabbage, broccoli and cauliflower need additional water while heads are developing. Vegetables that produce fruit or seedpods—beans, peas, corn, tomatoes, peppers and eggplant—require more water when they are flowering and setting fruit. In hot spells, tomatoes, eggplants and peppers, which are slow-maturing and deep-rooted, do better with a deep soaking once or twice a week.

Fertilizing. Mix a complete fertilizer (5-10-10, 10-10-10) into the soil at planting time (4 cups per 100 square feet). Use a water-soluble foliar fertilizer or manure tea to water in transplants. Depending on the type of crops you are growing, your soil and the type of fertilizer you are using, it may be necessary to repeat doses during the growing season.

When leafy vegetables show signs of poor leaf development, use a foliar fertilizer or manure tea. Fertilize other established vegetables by side-dressing: spread an even row of fertilizer down each side of a row or encircle each plant (1 to 2 pounds per 25-foot row or 1 to 2 tablespoons per plant). Work carefully into the soil and water thoroughly.

If you used a slow-release fertilizer at planting time, it may not be necessary to repeat feeding until midway through the growing season. On sandy soils, or in containers, giving plants repeated small doses of fertilizer will insure a steady supply.

Plants that take a long time to mature—tomatoes, eggplant, peppers, corn—are more demanding than lettuce or peas and beans (legumes). In cool weather, plants need a smaller amount of nutrients, as they grow slowly. In hot weather, do not fertilize on dry soils unless you can irrigate the garden, as the plants are unable to take up nutrients unless the soil is moist. Overfertilizing will cause salts to accumulate in the soil and damage plant roots.

Pest and disease control. Companion planting and crop rotation cut down on insect and disease problems. Annual vegetables and herbs should be rotated each year to avoid buildup in the soil of insects and diseases particular to some plants. This is difficult to accomplish in small gardens. Aromatic herbs and flowers, when planted among food crops, confuse marauding insects, distracting them from their normal diet of food crops. Radishes can be planted as a food crop to deter insects from other root crops. Plant lots of parsley to attract swallow-tail butterflies with enough left over for the kitchen. (For information on pest control, see Chapter 14.)

Fruits

Berry bushes, fruiting vines and fruit trees are sold bare-root, balled-and-burlaped or in containers and should be planted as any other shrub, vine or tree and should be spaced and sited according to recommendations. If space is limited, berry bushes and fruit trees can be trained as espaliers and grown on walls and fences. Dwarf fruit trees can be grown in containers.

Most fruit trees, vines and berry bushes prefer full sun. Exceptions are gooseberries and currants, cool-climate shrubs, which tolerate partial shade. In areas lacking the moist cool summers that they prefer, their roots benefit from heavy mulching and some shade from hot sun.

Chapter 9

Gardening in Containers

There is a great diversity of plants that can be grown in containers. In garden centers, on roof gardens and in shopping malls, mature trees and shrubs, as well as smaller plants, can be found growing happily in large tubs and planting boxes. Many of the plants found indoors are from the tropics where they flourish in the shade of taller forest plants, so they do well under limited light conditions. Out-of-door plants should be chosen for sunny or shady positions. They must be tolerant of local temperature fluctuations. Indoor and outdoor plantings can be seasonal or permanent. With judicious watering, fertilizing and pruning, even large plants can be maintained in containers indefinitely. For the average gardener, however, smaller moveable tubs and pots are more manageable.

Gardening in containers or pots lengthens the weeks when you can have bloom in your garden and broadens the choice of plants that you can grow. Doorways and windows, gateways and patios can be enlivened with changing displays in pots, window boxes and hanging baskets. Seasonal "dead" spaces in planting beds can be filled temporarily with pots of flowering annuals or perennials. Tender plants requiring winter protection can summer outdoors and be moved in later to shelter. Finicky plants with special soil or moisture requirements can be accommodated. For those who have only a balcony, a front stoop or access to a roof, this method may offer their only opportunities for growing plants.

Don't ignore large seasonal containers that remain out of doors during the winter. Plant bulbs in the fall to bloom in early spring before you replant and mulch the container for summer. Make arrangements with needle and broadleaf evergreen boughs by tucking them into the soil as you might arrange flowers in a vase. Add interesting bare branches, cones and seed heads. (See Chapter 11.)

Containers come in many sizes and shapes from pots and bowls to urns and jars, barrels and tubs, to window boxes. Choose them to harmonize with their setting and other nearby containers. They must be compatible in design with the plants they hold and be of suitable size to accommodate root growth. A container at least 18 inches in diameter or square is a good size for many plants or combinations of plants. Consider the ultimate size of the plants you want to install, their upright, rounded or weeping growth habits and the texture and color of the foliage and bloom. Group together in the same container plants with similar cultural requirements: sun or shade, dry or moist, rich or average, acid or alkaline soil.

Plant in the largest containers possible to decrease watering chores as the more soil and the deeper it is, the slower the container dries out. As plant foliage frequently covers much of the surface of the potting soil, realize that plants in pots may receive less rainwater than those in planting beds. Darker-colored containers will absorb more heat than lighter-colored ones and, while aiding the germination of seeds and hastening the growth of transplants, will need more watering if they are in direct sunlight. Unglazed terra-cotta pots are porous.

They appeal to those who like the look of natural materials but dry out more quickly than plastic pots.

All containers must have drainage holes, as plant roots will rot in wet soil. Plants sitting in saucers that fill up during a rain or from overwatering must be emptied frequently to avoid root rot. Filling the saucers with gravel or raising the container off the ground by setting it on the base of another upturned pot, a saucer turned upside down, bricks or narrow strips of flagstone, solves this problem while reducing insect access opportunities through the drainage holes.

For plants in containers, especially those standing in full sun, a layer of mulch on top of the soil will reduce evaporation from the soil surface, discourage weeds and keep water from heavy rains or hasty hand watering from washing the soil and splashing the plants with mud.

Set stakes and trellises for climbing plants, or those to be espaliered, at planting time to avoid damaging developing roots.

Deadhead and cut back annuals and perennials growing in containers to encourage rebloom and maintain attractive shapes. Treat deciduous and evergreen shrubs and small trees in containers as you would any others growing in the garden, pruning according to their blooming season, feeding as necessary and watching for and treating pest problems promptly.

In winter when the temperature is above freezing, lightly water plants overwintering outside to keep them from drying out, perhaps every two weeks.

As frequent watering leaches, or washes out, nutrients from the soil, plants growing in containers will need more frequent fertilizing than those in the ground. The less soil there is in the mix, the more fertilizer will be needed. Water-soluble and timed-release fertilizers are easiest to use. Water-soluble fertilizers can be diluted for more frequent applications. Timed-release fertilizers are dry granules that can be added to the potting mix at planting time as recommended on the package. The nutrients are released slowly over a long period of time. Begin to fertilize in spring and continue through the growing season. With permanent plantings, taper off as fall approaches so any late growth will harden off before winter.

Planting Containers

Select a container that provides insulation such as wood, terra cotta or fiberglass. Metal containers do not provide sufficient insulation; they allow freezing of roots and soil in winter and intense heat buildup in summer, especially in direct sunlight. Make sure there are adequate drainage holes. Add 2 inches of pebbles, gravel or pot shards to the bottom of the container to improve drainage. Cover with a piece of soil separator (a thin synthetic fabric designed to allow drainage) or several inches of salt hay or similar fine-textured material to prevent soil leakage. For soil, if planting annuals, perennials or vegetables, choose a good commercial potting mix, which will contain peat and perlite or vermiculite for good drainage, but will retain moisture long enough for the roots to absorb it and nutrients to help plants grow. Unlike garden soil, it will be free of weed seeds and soil-borne diseases. In large containers with more depth than required for good root development, fill excess space with commercial packaging peanuts or salt hay, packed down, before adding the soil.

Commercial potting soil requires yearly renewal because the wetting ingredient wears out, making watering increasingly difficult, and nutrients will have been used up or leached out. Refurbish soil in an established container by adding granular 5-10-5 and bonemeal, additional peat moss, compost or dehydrated manure and one-third new soil. Mix well.

If you mix your own potting soil, a good ratio is one part each of topsoil, peat moss, perlite (or builder's sand) and dehydrated cow manure. When planting a small tree or a shrub, add additional topsoil, up to one-third more, for extra stability. Mix well, and just before planting, stir in 5-10-5 granular fertilizer (3 to 4 trowels full per bushel of soil or the equivalent of another slow-release granular fertilizer). When planting vegetables, herbs or annuals, add an equal amount of bone meal or horticultural limestone.

To ensure winter hardiness when planting shrubs or small trees, select plants suitable for a colder climate (one to two zones north of your location). Lining large containers that winter out-of-doors with thin styrofoam sheeting will protect delicate roots.

Choose a container that will accommodate 3 or 4 extra inches of potting soil around the root ball. The container should be half again as deep as the root ball. If the container is too large, fill extra space with plastic peanuts or gravel. The top of the root ball should be 1 to 2 inches below the lip of the container.

If planting bare-root stock, which is available in late winter and early spring, trim roots back by one-third, branches by one-half. Spread the roots carefully over a mound of potting soil placed in the bottom of the container. Then fill in the container, lightly tamping down the soil as you go.

Plant suggestions for containers. For hot, dry positions, choose drought-tolerant plants: ornamental grasses, artemisia, sedums, rudbeckia, coreopsis, salvia, white marguerite, moss rose, nasturtium, cascading petunia, verbena, lantana, scented geranium, herbs such as fragrant hyssop, horehound, oregano, rosemary, sage and thyme.

For partly shady positions, try ageratum, begonia, browallia, impatiens, periwinkle *(Catharanthus rosea)*, nicotiana, fuchsia, and foliage plants including hosta, ferns, coleus and caladium.

Planting Hanging Baskets

Set the wire basket in a large pot or bucket to steady it. Line the basket with a 1-inch-thick layer of dampened sphagnum moss, and fill the center with good potting soil. Poke holes through the moss at the sides, and place plants through the holes into the soil. Next, plant the central section of the basket. Firm in well. Water in seedlings with a diluted solution of water-soluble fertilizer. Keep moss moistened at all times to provide humid air. Hanging baskets are exposed to the heat of the sun and drying winds on all sides and may need watering twice a day. Pinch back developing shoots to create a shapely and bushy plant.

Plant suggestions for hanging baskets. Some good choices are fuchsia, nasturtium, ivy-leafed geranium, impatiens, and cascading forms of begonia, verbena, petunia and lobelia. For foliage, try small-leaved ivy, vinca major, licorice plant *(Helichrysum petiolare)* and winged pea *(Lotus berthelotti)*.

Planting strawberry jars. Strawberry jars, glazed or unglazed terra-cotta urn-shaped jars with side-pocket planting holes, should be handled differently. Watering is difficult unless you make a central drainage core down the middle of the jar by inserting a 3- to 4-inch perforated polyvinyl pipe or by adding a 4-inch-wide center column of pebbles as you fill and plant the pot. Cover the jar's bottom drainage hole with screening. Cut the pipe several inches shorter than the height of the jar. The holes in the pipe should correspond as closely as possible with the planting holes. Stand the pipe upright in the jar, fill with pebbles and cover the top of the pipe with screening. Fill the jar with soil up to the lowest planting hole. Place the root ball of the plant into the planting pocket, drawing the roots carefully down into the jar. Add more soil around the roots and continue until the jar is filled. The jar must be in full light or rotated occasionally so all the plants gain the same exposure.

Plant suggestions for strawberry jars. Strawberry plants are traditional, but herbs, especially creeping thyme, and succulents (*Sedum* spp.), dwarf baby's breath (*Gypsophila repens*), alyssum and other small, textured trailing plants are equally satisfactory. The top of the pot can have an upright growing plant, even one trained on a stake or trellis if more height is desired.

Trough Gardens

Charming gardens can be made in weathered stone, cement or fiberglass troughs or sinks, either raised slightly off the ground for drainage or higher on legs of stones or bricks, or by setting the trough on a low wall. Because troughs and sinks are low in comparison to their length and width, they appear better balanced when filled with low plants. On sunny terraces, they are ideal for collections of dwarf rock garden or alpine plants. In shady spots, try dwarf spring bulbs and woodland plants (primrose, dogtooth violet, polypody fern, uvalaria). Cover the bottom of the trough with a thin layer of stone chips or gravel for drainage. Soil for alpines and succulents should be lean and gritty, and for woodland plants, use a rich potting soil with leaf mold added. Use a watering can with a fine rose attachment, and protect from cold winter winds and hot summer sun.

Dwarf Hardy Fruit Trees

An 18- to 24-inch tub is adequate for most dwarf fruit trees. Start young trees in a container just large enough to hold the roots after trimming off one-third of the strongest ones. Then each year after leaf fall, repot with fresh soil in a slightly larger container, again trimming back the roots. This combination of root trimming plus confining the roots in small containers "dwarfs" the plant, keeping it from developing fully. To assure winter survival, choose thick-walled containers with interior fiberglass or styrofoam lining, and select plants hardy to at least one zone north of your location.

Vegetables in Containers

A rule of thumb for ensuring enough room for root development when growing vegetables in containers is this: 6 inches minimum depth for lettuce; 8 to 12 inches for patio tomatoes, beets, radishes, onions, carrots, chard and spinach; and 12 to 24 inches for large tomatoes, eggplant, peppers, squash and cucumbers.

Chapter 10

Gardening with Roses

Roses are the most popular of all flowering shrubs. Next to tomato plants, they are probably planted by more gardeners than any other plant. You can choose roses for color, fragrance, minimum care requirements and hardiness. Some roses are recommended for hot, dry summers, some for hot and humid summers and some for cool ones. If there is a local rose society, or if your neighbors grow roses, they will be able to tell you what, if any, local problems are serious. For maintenance considerations, choose from newer varieties described as "disease-resistant," which are much less likely to be attacked by black spot, scale and other common rose diseases.

Roses are available bare-root during the winter or early spring, and they are available in containers later in the growing season. Buy bare-root plants from reputable mail-order suppliers or from local nurseries that specialize in roses. If container grown, buy healthy vigorous-looking plants. Choose those that are without damage or twiggy growth.

Many roses are grafted (a method of propagation). A grafted rose is a desirable rose growing on the stock or roots of another hardier variety. The graft will appear as a swelling on the stem above the roots of the growing stock and from which the canes of the top rose rise.

Roses do well in a wide range of soils but will perform best in deep loam, up to 2 feet, with a high humus content and a slightly acidic pH level—6.0 to 6.5. Roses need good drainage. Roses, especially hybrid teas, are frequently planted in separate gardens where their special requirements can be easily met. Many of the newer low-maintenance roses can be incorporated into mixed shrub and flower borders, into roadside plantings or used as ground covers.

Classifications of Roses

Roses are classified as *species roses* (wild), which naturalize easily, *shrub roses* (improved wild), *old garden roses* (roses introduced before 1867) and *modern roses*. Modern roses can also be classified by growth habit—shrub roses, climbers and ramblers.

Shrub roses include the following classifications:

- *Miniature:* usually very small floribunda, hybrid tea or natural climber, grown on their own root. Miniature roses are used for low hedges or are grown in containers.
- *Floribunda:* (about 3 feet) with medium-sized blossoms borne in clusters, frequently fragrant, medium-length stems, usually grafted.
- *Hybrid tea:* (4 to 5 feet) widely grown for the beauty of its blossoms, always grafted, usually grown in separate beds to simplify cultural requirements as they are prone to disease.
- *Grandiflora:* (up to 6 feet) flowers borne singly or in small clusters, with long stems, long blooming period, seldom fragrant, always grafted.
- *Tree rose:* any rose (usually hybrid tea or floribunda) grafted onto a tall trunk, or standard, more a form than a class of rose, maintained by special pruning techniques.

Climbing roses (6 to 20 feet) are not true climbers. They do not attach themselves with tendrils or rootlets, but, using their thorns for support, they do manage to clamber up into trees and shrubs. With assistance from eye screws and twine, those roses with stiff stems can be trained on walls and trellises or more formally on pillars. They are usually grafted and may have any type of flowers.

Rambling roses are roses with weak trailing or lax stems. They have very long, thin canes that bear thick clusters of small flowers. They can be trained on trellises but will naturally cascade over walls and fences or sprawl out as ground covers.

Current trends in rose growing include a renewed interest in old-fashioned species and shrub roses, including a new series of classic English roses developed by David Austin, bred, in general, toward more carefree, less disease-prone varieties. These are listed as "low-maintenance roses" or "hardy landscape roses." Among them are hardy hybrid *rosa rugosa* shrub roses and the Meidiland family of shrub roses, including varieties for mass plantings (ground-cover roses), hedges and to overhang walls or to cover slopes.

Rose Care

Planting. The same planting techniques apply to roses as to other shrubs (see Chapter 5). As soon as the soil is workable, plant bare-root roses in a hole large enough to accommodate the roots without crowding. If it is a grafted rose, set the graft 1 to 3 inches below the soil surface, depending on local winter temperatures. Place roots over a mound of soil formed in the bottom of the hole. Pack soil carefully over roots by hand. Water in when hole is half filled to settle soil. Complete filling and water plant again. Mulch well after rose is established.

Remove a potted rose from its container carefully with as little disturbance to its root ball as possible. The planting hole will have to be deep enough to allow the top of the graft union to rest below the finished surface of the soil.

When planting a boxed rose, carefully remove the plant from the container. Soak the root ball in a bucket of water for several hours. Gently

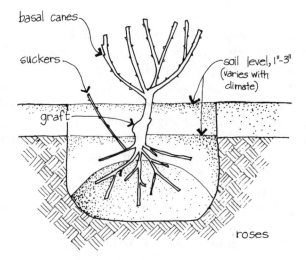

remove the soiless mix, or packing, from around the roots, and plant as described above. A boxed rose can also be planted "as is" in its box. It will need frequent watering during the first season as it will wilt easily.

Pruning. Prune most roses (including species, miniatures, floribunda, hybrid tea and grandiflora) before they bloom, in early spring as soon as leaf buds begin to swell. Prune to maintain the desired height and shape of the plant and to keep the center of the shrub open for good air circulation. Early pruning stimulates vigorous growth from the base of the plant, and this kind of growth produces the branches with the most flowers. Remove all dead, weak, diseased and crossing wood; cut all remaining canes back by one-third. Make all cuts on a slant $1/4$ inch above a strong and preferably outside bud to encourage new growth to develop outward.

Suckers, which arise from the root system below the graft union of a grafted plant, should be removed. Eventually, they will crowd out the more desirable rose on top. (Do not confuse them with new basal canes rising from above the graft.)

Treat rambler and climbing roses as follows: Climbers, which have vigorous, thick, stiff canes may bloom once a year or repeatedly into fall. In spring, cut back all small laterals on all climbers by two-thirds. With climbers that bloom repeatedly, remove one-third of the longest, oldest canes at the same time to make way for new canes sprouting from the base. Climbers that bloom only once a year can be thinned after bloom. Ramblers, which have thinner, lax canes, bloom only once a year. They should have their laterals pruned back by two-thirds in spring. After bloom, prune out all dead wood. On vigorously growing roses, remove one-third of the long, oldest canes at the base of the plant, less on weaker plants.

When new growth appears on climbers and ramblers, let it harden before tying as it will be brittle and break easily. Canes that grow out in awkward directions should be removed.

Prune neglected and overgrown climbers and ramblers before they leaf out in spring, even if this means sacrificing some bloom the current year.

When cutting roses for flower arrangements, cut in late afternoon or early morning. Choose flowers that are just opening or are half opened. Cut at a 45° angle just above a five-leaflet leaf that is outwardly facing. New growth will begin from the base of the leaf and develop in an outward direction. Limit the amount of foliage you cut from newly planted roses for the first two to three years to allow them to become firmly established.

Fertilizing. Roses need heavy fertilizing. Feed species and shrub roses, as well as old roses and climbers, once in the spring as they break dormancy. Feed climbers again after first bloom. Modern hybrid tea roses and roses growing in containers should be fed every three to five weeks. Use either dry or liquid forms of a complete rose fertilizer and apply according to directions. Apply on moist soil and water in to speed fertilizer to the roots of the plant.

Feed newly planted roses about a month after planting, when they have become established. Feed newly pruned roses when new foliage appears.

In areas with cold winter temperatures, stop feeding all roses six weeks before the first expected frost date to allow time for new growth to harden.

Maintenance. All roses need some care. Keep the areas under plants free of fallen leaves and twigs to discourage pest problems. Water well (1 to 2 inches a week in dry spells). Watch for and treat pest problems promptly. In cold climates, mulch roses heavily in winter to protect the graft area. Encircle the plant with a cylinder of wire mesh and fill with dried leaves or dirt, or simply mound dirt up (10 to 12 inches) around the plant. In spring, slowly remove the mulch as the weather warms.

In exposed areas, cut back tall rose canes in late fall to keep them from whipping about in the wind. Check loose fasteners on all bushes growing on walls and fences.

Roses growing in containers must receive special protection in cold areas as the soil in the container will get much colder than that around plants set in the ground. Move container (plant and all) into an unheated basement, garage or root cellar.

Chapter 11

Gardening with Bulbs

Bulbs, corms, rhizomes, tuberous roots and tubers are referred to here jointly as *bulbs*. They are all plants that form swollen underground storage roots. Many contain enough stored food and moisture to sustain growth for a year, needing only warmth, additional moisture and light to begin growth and to flower, a process which many can complete very rapidly. Bulbs have adapted to survive inhospitable cold and drought conditions in their native habitats. Knowledge of the climate in the place of their origin will provide clues as to which bulbs will prosper in your garden.

Most of the hardiest spring bulbs, snowdrops (*Galanthus*), Dutch crocus (*Crocus vernus*), some scilla, trillium and most daffodils and lilies, are native to regions with wet winters, freezing temperatures and frequent snow cover and cool moist summers. They can withstand being frozen and require, or can tolerate, rain in summer.

Most other crocuses, bulbous iris, many fritillaria, most tulips and some colchicum and eremurus are native to areas with cold winters but dry summers, so they need protection from wet in summer and profit from summer shade or overplanting with drought-tolerant perennials. They will be damaged or destroyed by automatic watering systems that negate the required dry dormant season.

Perhaps the greatest number of well-known bulbs are native to South Africa with mild winters and long dry summers. They include gladiolus, freesia, sparaxis, tritonia, ixia, babiana, *Lachenalia*, amaryllis, clivia and agapanthus. These are tender bulbs that must be heavily mulched, lifted and stored or be grown indoors in colder climates.

Daffodil is the common name for the genus *Narcissus*. In the South, the term "jonquil" is frequently used to refer to all daffodils. The many hybrids of daffodils are classified by the characteristics of the form of the flower and the shape and length of the cup: trumpet, large cup, small cup, double, triandrus, cyclamineus, jonquilla, tazetta, poeticus, species and wild forms, split corona and miniature. Daffodils vary in hardiness. They need a cold dormant period which explains the need to buy "precooled" bulbs if you live in the South.

Siting Bulbs in the Garden

Bulbs are often grown in bulb beds and followed by summer- blooming perennials or ornamental grasses. They are added to shrub borders where their untidy ripening foliage can be easily hidden. Snowdrops, spring snowflakes and some crocus species lend themselves to naturalizing in the lawn as their leaves die down before the lawn requires mowing. Daffodils, summer snowflakes, fritillarias, species tulips, martigon

lilies and camassias (one of the few bulbs that will grow in wet places) can be planted in woodland gardens or rough grass, which must not be mowed until the bulbs go dormant. Fall crocus and colchicum, which flower before the leaves emerge, follow in the fall. Hardy and tender bulbs can be grown in containers to be brought to flower outdoors or indoors.

Most bulbs prefer a sandy, neutral, well-drained soil. Avoid heavy clay or hardpan since poor drainage and excessive moisture cause rot. In overly moist areas, bulbs can be planted in raised beds.

Make a plan of your garden when the bulbs are in bloom, recording their location, varieties and colors. Mark spots in the garden where you would like to plant more because, when planting time comes around in the fall, it is difficult to remember just where you meant to put them. In mass plantings, the smaller the bulb, the greater the number required for maximum effect.

Choose bulbs that are firm and unblemished, without signs of insect damage. They should be moist and feel heavy for their size, indicating they have not dried out. Larger bulbs will produce larger or more numerous flowers.

When to Plant Bulbs

Plant newly purchased bulbs as soon as possible since they lose viability the longer they are out of the ground. If necessary, put bulbs in paper bags and store in a cool place, such as the refrigerator, until you are ready to plant.

Most bulbs should be planted when dormant: in early autumn for spring-flowering bulbs to allow roots to develop before the ground freezes, or early spring for summer-flowering ones. Spring- flowering bulbs can be dug and divided just after bloom when you can find them easily. They can be replanted immediately or stored for planting in the fall. Exceptions are snowdrops and snowflakes, which establish easily if transplanted in or just after bloom. Tulips can be dug and stored during the summer to protect them from moisture.

As a general rule, the smaller hardy bulbs, including spring crocus, aconite, chionodoxa, scilla and hyacinth, are planted in early fall, followed by daffodils, to allow time for root development before winter. Tulips are planted in late fall up until the ground freezes as they do not develop roots until spring.

Lilies, which never go completely dormant, are planted in early summer and will probably have actively growing roots. They should be planted immediately, or kept in slightly damp peat moss until planting time. An exception is the madonna lily, which is available for planting in the fall.

Tender bulbs, such as gladiolus, dahlia and tuberous begonia, are planted in late spring, after the last frost, and dug and stored in late fall in colder areas. Caladium and begonia tubers can be started indoors. Plant them 1 inch deep, on their sides, with their buds or "eyes" up, in flats with a soil mix of equal parts moist sphagnum moss, compost and sharp sand to which superphosphate or bulb food has been added; water well, and keep at 75° F. When small leaves have formed, plant in the garden, 1 inch deep at intervals of 8 inches for best coverage.

Fall crocus and colchicum are planted in late summer for fall bloom. Colchicum will blossom on the windowsill without soil or water. Then they can be set out in the garden for showy foliage in the spring. (For information on how to plant bulbs, see Chapter 5.)

Caring for Bulbs in the Garden

If the winter has been dry or the spring without rain, water spring bulb beds thoroughly and deeply and continue to water until the foliage begins to yellow, signalling the onset of dormancy. During this time, bulbs are building up food reserves for the next year. Fertilize bulbs as they begin to emerge and again after bloom with a slow-release fertilizer low in nitrogen and high in potassium and phosphate, 5-10-10 or "bulb booster," to encourage root and bud growth while avoiding excessive leaf development.

Like perennials, most bulbs die down after the growth cycle is completed and return the following year. When bulbs have finished blooming, remove the blossom heads to prevent seed production, which weakens the bulb. As all bulbs restore themselves through their foliage, the foliage must be left to turn yellow and wither naturally at which time it will pull easily from the bulb. Do not braid foliage or tie in clumps as sunlight will be prevented from reaching the center of the clump. For the same reason, when cutting lilies, do not remove more than one-third of the leafy stem. Bulbs can be overplanted with the larger perennials or other ground covers to hide yellowing foliage. Choose drought-tolerant species to avoid the need for heavy summer watering, which may cause bulb rot.

Planting Bulbs in Containers

Bulbs can be planted in containers in soil for use outdoors or indoors. For continuous bloom, plant bulbs at two-week intervals from early to late fall, and try early and late varieties. Choose containers that drain well. Cover the drain holes with window screening, soil separator or pot shards and fill partially with soil mix. Use a commercial planting mix or a mixture of equal parts garden loam, builder's sand and peat moss or ground bark. Set bulbs so that tips are level with the rim of the container. Bulbs can be closely packed so long as they do not touch each other or the side of the container. Add soil until the bulbs are barely covered. Water well to settle. Place in a cool, protected spot until bulbs root (fourteen to fifteen weeks). Containers can also be set in a trench in the garden and covered with a thick leaf or straw mulch to prevent freezing. Keep evenly moist. When bulbs are well-rooted and sprouts are showing green (six to eight weeks), bring the container into warmth (60° F) and light for an additional three to four weeks to force bloom. Support floppy foliage with plant rings or twiggy branches tucked in the dirt around the rim of the pot.

Interesting arrangements can be made in large, deep containers by mixing groups of different bulbs. Set those requiring the most depth first, add soil to cover and follow with small bulbs set closer to the soil surface. Leave enough room below the rim for mulching and watering. Decorate large containers in the garden with broad and needle evergreen boughs during the winter months as they wait for spring.

Forcing Bulbs in Water

Tender daffodil cultivars (i.e. 'Paperwhites', 'Tazetta'), frequently referred to as "narcissus," crocus, hyacinths and amaryllis, are used for forcing in water indoors in northern climates.

Narcissus: Plant bulbs from fall through early winter. Fill two-thirds of a shallow bowl with pebbles. Set narcissus bulbs, barely touching each other, with their flat sides toward the rim. Mounding some gravel up around the bulbs will help to anchor them. Add water and maintain at a level just below the base of the bulb as its rests on the pebbles. Set bulbs in a cool dark spot until growth begins. Then bring into the light and warmth to force flowering.

Dutch hyacinth, crocus and amaryllis: Set bulbs, individually, in narrow-necked jars that are made especially for water culture. (The narrow neck supports the bulb above the water, and the space below provides sufficient room for root development.) Add a piece of activated charcoal to the water to prevent algae growth. A narrow strip of florist's clay, placed in a ring around the bulb as it rests on the glass, will prevent amaryllis bulbs from toppling over when in bloom. Add water until it barely touches the base of the bulb. Place the containers in a cool dark place for a few weeks until roots are well developed and leaves appear. Bring crocus into bright light and warmth when buds are a couple of inches high. Hyacinths may take up to five weeks for the flower buds to reach about 4 inches and be visible through the leaf sheaths. Check the water level every few days throughout the flowering period. Compost spent bulbs. Bulbs forced in water will not bloom again.

Storing Bulbs

Bulbs are dug and stored to protect them from cold, heat or moisture. In northern climates, tender bulbs are dug to protect them from freezing. In southern climates, hardy bulbs cannot remain in the ground year-round because the temperature never drops low enough to induce dormancy. Dig bulbs carefully with a spading fork and allow any remaining soil to dry on the bulb when it will become easy to shake off. Remove dried leaves and discard soft bulbs. Do not separate bulbs that have developed offsets before storing. Wait until replanting time to avoid their drying out. Store each variety, carefully labeled, in a loose medium such as vermiculite, perlite, sand or peat moss to prevent them from touching each other to reduce the spread of disease. It is not necessary to dust bulbs with a fungicide or insecticide unless you have had a problem with narcissus bulb flies or gladiolus thrips.

Gladiolus, crocosmia, trigridia, freesia, *Achimenes* and *Hymenocallis,* which have harder shells, should be stored in net bags and hung in a cool dry location. More succulent bulbs, dahlia, calla, carma, *Orithogalum* and gloriosa lily, should be stored in a loose medium to which a few drops of water can be added occasionally to prevent them from drying out completely.

Clivia, agapanthus and crinum are evergreen bulbs. They need light and water during winter. Plant them in containers so they can be brought indoors during cold periods. Deciduous bulbs in containers can be stacked and stored away from freezing temperatures to be started again next growing season.

Chapter 12

Starting Seeds

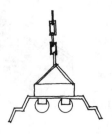

Most vegetables and annual flowers are started from seed. These seeds can be divided into three groups: hardy, half-hardy and tender, based on their ability to germinate and grow under certain soil and moisture conditions. Hardy seeds can be planted in open ground as soon as the ground can be worked in the spring. Some can be broadcast on late snows. Half-hardy seeds can be sown after all danger of frost has passed. Tender seeds require warm soil conditions. These are frequently started indoors and set out when the soil has thoroughly warmed up.

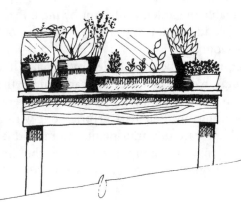

For all seeds, read the instructions on the seed package that give germination periods and requirements, whether they need light or darkness for germination, transplanting times and other pertinent information. When seeds are started indoors, avoid leggy or overgrown seedlings by adding the hardening- off period to the germination and growing times and start seed according to the last frost date in your region.

Sowing Indoors

Commercial starter kits, consisting of a simple or divided shallow drainage tray and a clear plastic cover, are available, or you can make your own kit from any clean, shallow, plastic or styrofoam tray, using plastic wrap or plastic bags for covers. If you lack windowsill space, various forms of indoor lighting setups make seed-starting and nursing tender plants possible in dark basements.

Fill a planting flat with moistened, commercially prepared, sterilized seed-starting mix. Mix small seeds with sand to insure even distribution. Broadcast or sow the seeds in shallow furrows. Tiny seeds will fall in the crevices. Cover larger seeds with fine soil or vermiculite. Mist gently if soil has dried out. Label each flat with the name of the plant and the date sown. Since germination times differ, plant only one kind of seed in each flat. Cover the flat with a piece of glass or plastic wrap. Or create a small greenhouse by placing a plant label at each corner of the flat and slipping the flat into a plastic bag. Unless otherwise specified, maintain the temperature between 70° and 75° F, the average for germinating most seeds. If the temperature is lower than recommended, use heater 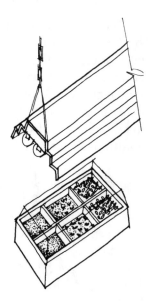 cables or a heating mat, available in garden centers or by mail. Place flat away from direct light. If condensation appears, open and air out the flat for several hours to avoid rot.

The first leaflike structures to appear are called *cotyledon*. They are followed by the first true leaves. When they appear, remove the covers, and move the flats to indirect sunlight and cooler temperatures, 65° to 70° F. Thin seedlings in their flats or prick out with a pencil point or tip of a label and carefully transplant into individual containers. Keep the planting mixture barely moist. When the first true leaves have opened fully, begin fertilizing every two weeks with water-soluble 10-10-10.

Damping off is caused by fungi that may be present in the soil, the seeds themselves or in the water, and results in the sudden wilting and dying of otherwise healthy looking seedlings. It is most likely to occur when soil and air temperatures are above 68° F. To avoid damping off, do not overwater seedlings. Thin out new seedlings as soon as they emerge and before they become crowded. Use a sterile growing medium with good drainage and never soil collected from your garden. Use clean seed flats. Drench seed flat and soil medium with a weak fungicide solution (¹/₂ teaspoon per gallon of water) before seeding.

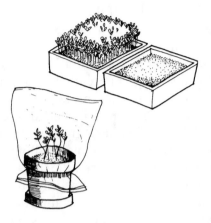

Hardening Off

Seedlings grown indoors or purchased from a greenhouse or garden center should be conditioned before being planted in the garden. To acclimatize seedlings to greater fluctuations of temperature and light, set them in a cold frame for seven to ten days, or set flats outside in a protected spot for an hour the first day, and gradually lengthen the time each day thereafter.

Transplanting Seedlings to the Garden

Transplant seedlings when they fill their containers but before they become top-heavy or begin blooming. If the soil in the planting bed is dry, thoroughly dampen it a day in advance. Moisten the seedlings, or transplants, before removing them from the container. Run a knife around inside the rim and tap the container sharply on a hard surface. Turn the plant out into the palm of your hand with the stem between your fingers to catch and retain as much soil as possible. If the root system of a seedling has filled the container, be sure to loosen any encircling roots at the bottom and side surfaces by pulling them gently away from the dirt mass and spreading them out in a hole large enough not to cramp them. When setting out seedlings in a peat pot, remove the top inch of the pot and set soil in the pot evenly with the soil in the bed. Set the seedlings at recommended intervals at the same soil depth at which they had been growing, backfill, gently firm in and water well. Water in vegetable seedlings with a 10 percent solution of water-soluble fertilizer. Pinch back top growth of annual and perennial seedlings to encourage root growth and bushiness. Try to plant on an overcast day, and shade seedlings from direct sun (or late frosts) for several days with baskets, planting trays or newspapers.

Sowing Outdoors

In well-prepared soil, make a furrow with the back of a rake or the tip of a trowel, or outline a prepared area with pebbles or flat sticks and broadcast seeds therein. Plant seeds at the depth recommended on the seed package. Or, in cool weather, plant seeds to a depth approximately three times the thickness of the seed lying down in the soil. Increase this to four times in warm weather. Mix fine seed with sand for even distribution. Cover seed with fine soil to the suggested depth and tamp down lightly with a rake or the palm of your hand. Keep seed beds moist at all times with a fine mist so as not to dislodge the seed until germination is complete.

Biennials are easy to start from seed but require slightly different handling. Seed is sown during the summer, in a cold frame, if possible, or in another protected spot. Seedlings are set out in the fall or, if tender, potted up and carried over in the frame until the following spring.

Many perennials can be started from seed, but others have become so highly developed that they may not produce seed, or not come true from seed. It is necessary to reproduce these plants vegetatively, by division or cuttings.

Saving Seeds

You can collect and save your own seeds. Some seeds will separate easily from the plant when ripe. Pick or shake them into a paper bag or envelope. Those in pods will rattle when ripe. If they are in wet pulp (i.e., tomatoes, peppers, cucumbers, etc.), separate them from the pulp as completely as possible (fruit should be very ripe), and leave them to dry on screens or paper towels. Store seeds, carefully marked, sealed in jars or plastic bags in a dry cool place until planting time. Use seeds as soon as possible as some cease to be viable after a year.

It is one thing to collect wild seeds; it is another thing to collect modern hybrid vegetable and garden flower seeds. In the past, all seeds were open-pollinated, mostly by insects, and bred true to the plant, or plants, that were their parents. To be sure that next year's crop will be like its predecessor, you and your nearby neighbors can grow only one variety of each flower and vegetable. Otherwise, chances are they will be cross-pollinated and different from what you expect. Within plant families, there are few restrictions: melons and pumpkins, red and green lettuces, carrots and weedy cousins can mix.

Seed production is a very specialized process. Modern hybrids are hand pollinated and should be obtained from seed companies each year. Saving seeds from hybrids is generally unsuccessful because the second generation will probably be very different from and inferior to the first. Also, some seeds are treated against viruses. That treatment will not carry over to a second generation of seeds.

Chapter 13

Propagating Plants

Starting trees and shrubs from seed is not only time consuming, but there is no guarantee that the resulting plant will resemble the parent. Unless seed is produced under carefully controlled conditions, the seedlings may not grow true to the parent but may differ radically. A quicker and surer method is to increase your plant stock vegetatively, by division, softwood and hardwood cuttings or by layering. These methods will give you an exact copy of the original plant.

Division

Plants that have multiple basal stems can usually be divided into two or more sections. Make sure that each section has some root, stem and foliage. Divide only healthy, strongly growing plants. When planting out any division, prepare the planting site well in advance by digging and working peat moss, compost or leaf mold, and sand (if the soil is heavy and drainage poor) into the existing soil.

Perennials

Cut a circle around the plant with a digging fork. Get under and lift the entire mass. Cut or gently pull apart the crowded clumps into two or more sections.

Discard the woody central portion and any diseased or stunted parts. Cut the tops back to 6 inches. Replant the healthy divisions, and water well to settle. In general, divide spring- and summer-blooming perennials in the late summer or fall; divide fall- and winter-blooming perennials in the spring. Many can be divided in either spring or fall. Among perennials that can be divided easily are aloe, hybrid astilbe, bleeding heart, coralbell, coreopsis, daylily, hosta, monarda, mint, peony and shasta daisy.

Ground Covers

Cut a 6-inch piece of the plant that includes a portion of its root system. Dip it in a rooting hormone, shaking off any excess, and plant it to fill in bare spots in existing beds or to start new beds. Mulch large areas in advance and set ground-cover divisions through the mulch at 8-inch intervals and at the same depth at which they were previously growing. Easy ground covers to divide are ajuga, *Astilbe pumila*, epimedium, Japanese and Allegheny pachysandra, European and Canadian ginger and sweet woodruff.

Shrubs

Divide multistemmed shrubs or shrubs that spread by stolons by pushing a sharp spade down to both sever and lift a portion of the plant or dig up the entire plant, cutting or sawing through the root system, and replant each individual healthy section. Shrub forms of dogwood, forsythia, inkberry *(Ilex glabra)*, lilac and some mahonias can be propagated by this method.

Cuttings

Softwood

Many ornamental trees and shrubs are easy to propagate from herbaceous or softwood cuttings taken from new stems just as they are beginning to harden. Cuttings should be taken from healthy plants growing in a normal manner, not from those under stress of drought or disease. Cleanliness, both of your cutting implement and planting containers, and not allowing the cuttings to dry at any time are keys to success. Easy to root are butterfly bush, cherry, cotoneaster, crape myrtle, deutzia, lilac, spirea, stewartia, viburnum, witch hazel and small-leaved rhododendron and azalea. Softwood stem cuttings from chrysanthemum can be taken in the spring as the plants begin new growth, from candytuft, *Phlox divaricata* and *Phlox sublata* and other rock garden plants as they finish blooming.

To test for readiness of softwood cuttings: Toward the end of spring, bend a piece of this year's plant growth at the end of a branch or twig. If it snaps, it is ready. If it bends over but remains limp, wait a week and try again. It will come clean without attached bark. To prevent the cuttings from drying, place in a dark plastic bag and, if necessary, temporarily store, tightly closed, in a dark cool spot, even a picnic cooler with ice, but do not freeze. To hold and root your cuttings, prepare an 8-inch shallow bulb pan or small flat, with a drainage hole, filled with a well-moistened rooting mix of equal parts sphagnum peat moss and perlite, or builder's sand, at least 3 inches deep. Alternatively, for just a few cuttings, start them in individual $2\frac{1}{2}$- to 3-inch containers that are easy to handle, set together in a portable flat.

Take the cuttings in early morning when the wood is full of moisture. Snap or cut off the new growth. Remove all but two to five leaves at the tip of the branch. This will reduce the strain on the cutting from moisture loss due to transpiration. To make your final cuts, use a clean, sharp single-edge razor blade to cut pieces 4 to 6 inches long, or, if the parent plant growth is short, 2 to 3 inches. Cut at a 60° angle, just below a leaf node. Immediately dip the stem end of the cutting in a root-inducing hormone powder (available at garden centers), gently shaking off any excess. Make a hole in the rooting medium with a pencil. Insert stem about 1 to 3 inches into the rooting mix.

Space cuttings about 2 to 4 inches apart. With large-leaved plants (rhododendron, viburnum), it may be necessary to cut back each leaf by half to avoid overlap. When all the cuttings are inserted, water gently to settle mix around the base of each cutting. Water should drain from the base of the pan. To maintain high humidity, create a tent over the cuttings with a polyethylene bag (food storage bag, bread wrapper) using plant labels or short sticks around the edge of the pan to suspend the plastic so it doesn't sit on the foliage. Secure tightly with a rubber band. Set the rooting pan or flat on several bricks or small stones in a location with bright light but no direct sun. After four weeks, remove the plastic bag and tug gently at several cuttings. If they resist, rooting has begun. If not, replace the bag and try again in ten days. To acclimatize the cuttings once they have rooted, poke several holes into the plastic bag. Several days later, poke some more holes. After ten days to two weeks, remove the bag, leaving the container in the same place, and water if necessary.

In early fall, discard weak, less vigorous cuttings and pot up remaining ones in individual containers, 2½ to 3 inches in diameter, with drainage holes, using a good commercial potting mix. Once they have rooted, they will require protection through their first winter. House them in a location where they will not receive heat from winter sun, which can cause alternate freezing and thawing, damaging the plants. Ideal locations are a cold frame, a window well under a plexiglass cover or in a crate wrapped in a white polyethylene trash bag and set on the north side of a building or under a heavily needled spruce tree. Allow the soil to freeze naturally and to stay frozen until the weather warms in spring.

In early spring, open the cold frame or remove the trash bag so the plants don't push new growth, which may be nipped by a late frost. Once the temperature has normalized and new growth starts, the plants can be set out in the garden or a nursery bed.

Hardwood

Hardwood cuttings are taken from mature wood, the previous season's growth, while the plant is dormant, from late fall through the winter. If the plant is deciduous, take cuttings after the leaves have fallen. Some popular plants that can be reproduced by hardwood cuttings are abelia, boxwood, gardenia, mock orange and lavender.

Take cuttings 6 to 10 inches long with three to four buds per section. Cut at a 60° angle just below a bud at the bottom of each cutting. Several cuttings can be obtained from a long stem. In this case, cut the top end at right angles just above a bud so you will know "which end is up."

In mild winter climates, cuttings can be planted out immediately. Prepare a narrow trench about 8 inches deep. Cover the bottom with an inch of sand. Dip the base of the cuttings in a rooting hormone powder. Set the cuttings 3 to 6 inches apart in the trench, leaning them against the side. Fill in the trench with moderately fertile garden soil mixed with vermiculite or perlite. Leave only the section with the top bud protruding from the trench. The other buds will make roots. Do not add fertilizer. Allow 2 feet between rows. Top growth should show after several weeks. Early the following spring, cut back hard to encourage bushy growth. By summer or early fall, new shrubs will be ready to set out in permanent positions.

In colder regions, tie cuttings together in conveniently sized bundles, carefully labeled, with butt ends even, and bury bundles in a flat facing in the same direction. A good medium is 1 part peat moss and 3 parts sand or course perlite, slightly moist. Store in a cool cellar (40° to 45° F). Or cuttings can be buried out-of-doors in a cold frame in sand or light sandy, well-drained soil below frost line. A callus will form over each butt end. In early spring when the ground is workable, take cuttings from storage, dip base in rooting hormone and plant out in nursery rows or containers. Set cuttings so only the tip shows above soil. Cuttings with a large number of buds can be set with one-third of the stem protruding from the soil. By fall, cuttings should be well rooted and ready to transplant to their permanent site. Test for rooting by tugging gently on the cutting every few weeks. Some hardwood cuttings may take as long as a year to root. When ready, the cuttings will have well-branched roots, forming a dense root ball about 2 inches in diameter.

Layering

During spring and summer, layer woody-stemmed shrubs (azalea, barberry, berry bushes, clematis, dogwood, forsythia, grape, lilac, rose, Russian olive, winter jasmine, wisteria, viburnum), which have a tendency to root readily when their branches come in contact with the soil. Layering is the formation of roots along a stem while the stem is still attached to the parent plant.

Tip layering. Berry bushes, such as blackberry, loganberry and raspberry, can be propagated in late summer. Select a supple stem of this year's growth and bend it to the ground, inserting the tip end into a previously dug 4-inch-deep hole. Cover it with soil to hold it in place and water it well. Roots will form and a new shoot will develop in a few weeks. In late fall or early spring, dig up and transplant the new berry bush.

Simple layering. In spring or late fall, select a one-year-old, dormant flexible lower branch. The bark should be scraped or notched about 18 inches from the tip at the spot where the branch will come in contact with the soil. Bend the branch until the exposed area meets the soil. Remove any foliage that might be buried. Dust the scraped area

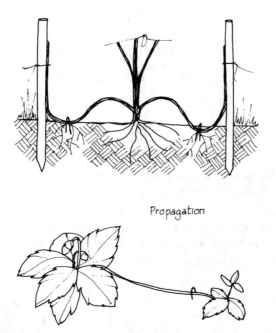

Propagation

with rooting hormone. Dig a small trench and bury the prepared area of the branch in the trench with the tip pointing upwards and exposed. Keep the branch in place with a forked stick, bent wire or small stone. Cover the contact area with a layer of soil. Keep the root area damp. The new roots will form on the buried bend. Check by sticking your fingers in the soil. When the layer has rooted, it can be severed from its parent plant. (It may take up to a year.) When well established the following spring, transplant to its new location.

Chapter 14

Controlling Insects
and Disease

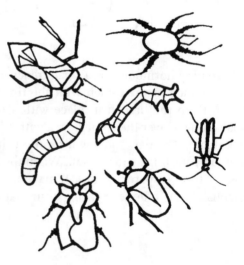

A garden with a diverse population of plants is more resistant to insects and disease than a monoculture—a crop of a single species—as it avoids the build-up a particular pest. Even so, all gardens suffer attacks at one time or another, often mild, sometimes severe, of some form of pest problem. As plants are more susceptible to insects and diseases when they are under stress, you should make every effort to maintain the health of your plants with healthy gardening practices. This means keeping a neat and clean garden, planting disease-resistant varieties (especially in the vegetable garden) and observing the proper spacing, siting and installation of plants. The correct maintenance of your plants, fertilizing, watering and mulching, as well as the timing of pruning to shape or remove diseased and damaged branches that can harbor insects, play a role in the prevention and control of pest problems.

In the past, heavy use of toxic chemicals resulted in great environmental damage, the poisoning of people, of wild and domestic animals, of birds, butterflies and beneficial insects and the contamination of foods and underground water supplies. Meanwhile, the pests have become increasingly immune to the pesticides. Secondary pests appear when organisms that keep them in check are eliminated.

Fertilizers as well may contain chemicals and should be applied with caution. Runoff due to rain or watering may carry fertilizers into nearby natural streams and ponds, causing pollution and algae build-up. Excessive application of nitrogen causes succulent growth, which attracts some pests, is weak under stress from strong winds and is easily damaged by frost.

Integrated Pest Management. An alternative and more enlightened approach to a healthy garden is called Integrated Pest Management, or IPM. IPM stresses sound cultural practices and the switch to natural and biological controls. If you are concerned about the use of dangerous pesticides, by monitoring your garden year-round and checking regularly for the appearance of insects and diseases and by identifying key pests and observing pest-prone plants, you can handle the majority of pest problems without resorting to environmentally unfriendly or hazardous treatments.

The key to controlling pest problems and avoiding serious damage lies in the correct identification of the problem and treating it promptly, before it becomes a major problem. Are you dealing with an insect, a plant disease, or are the symptoms caused by environmental stress?

Total eradication of an insect is no longer the goal. Rather, management should be your focus, reducing the insect population to acceptable levels. Treatment will be based in part on your level of tolerance of the damage being done to your plants, so a few chewed leaves may not necessitate any treatment. Your garden will benefit best from early detection and spot treatment of infected plants.

Nontoxic Controls

Beneficial "bugs." Not all bugs are bad. Recognize and protect natural predatory insects that feed on aphids, scale insects, mites, soil-dwelling boring insects, caterpillars, worms and other plant pests. They include pollinating bees, green lacewings, ladybugs, spined soldier bugs and other helpful beetles, praying mantis, and trichogramma and other wasps.

Some of these beneficial insects can be purchased through the mail, but will migrate from your garden as their food supply diminishes. Provide them with other protein sources (pollen and nectar) once the "bad" bugs have been consumed. Be wary of any chemicals that may upset the fragile balance between "good" bugs and "bad" bugs.

Plant strong-smelling herbs (catnip, dill, garlic, hyssop, mint, rosemary, rue, savory) and flowers (calendulas, marigolds, nasturtiums, petunias), which seem to have insect-repellent properties, among other plants to control garden insects. Leave a few plants favored by the "bad" bugs to lure them away from your more treasured ones. Plant flowers (sunflowers, thistles, black-eyed Susan, clover) and fruiting shrubs and trees that attract birds (and pollinating bees) who will consume quantities of insects.

Manual controls. Use mechanical devices, including traps and deterrents against flying insects: sticky papers and disks, sticky substances applied in bands around tree trunks, tree wrap and beetle traps. Use fine mesh and landscape fabrics (geotextiles) to protect fruits and vegetables from birds and egg-laying flying insects.

Spread diatomaceous earth (used in swimming-pool filters), ashes, sand, pine-needle mulch, tar paper and cutworm collars to deter crawling insects.

Infestations of aphids, mites and many other small insects can be washed off with a strong blast of water from the garden hose. Hand pick large bugs. Prune out branches and twigs heavily infested with egg nests. If only a few leaves on a plant are infected by a disease, pick them off by hand and destroy.

Biological controls. If these methods aren't sufficient, the next step is to use biological controls. Each year, there are more and more organic pest controls on the market that are not damaging to the environment. Their ingredients are found in plants, among them pyrethrum, citrus, neem, cashew and pawpaw.

Bacterial controls include *Bacillus thuringiensis*, or Bt, which is safe for humans and lethal to moth and butterfly larvae. Appearing under such trade names as Dipel, Thuricide and Attack, this bacterial control is a soluble powder that is mixed with water and sprayed on infected plants, including valuable fruit and vegetable crops. *Bacillus polilliae* has been used extensively against the grubs of Japanese beetles. These soil organisms—which are actually diseases—enter the insect through the mouth, multiply in the bloodstream and kill it.

Beneficial nematodes (minute worms) attack parasitic nematodes that feed on plant roots. Beneficial nematodes are a safe biological control for sow bugs, pill bugs, earwigs, onion maggots and other root weevils. Adding quantities of organic fertilizer will nurture the population of beneficial nematodes as well as bolster the health of your plants. Rotate crops to avoid a heavy build-up of plant-eating nematodes, which favor a specific plant.

Pheromones, which are secretions emitted by insects for the purpose of communicating with other insects of the same species, have been synthesized and are used to lure insects to traps or poisonous baits. While they trap only a portion of the targeted insect, they do monitor the presence of that insect in the area.

Hormones, present in sprays known as "growth regulators," control an insect's ability to grow or reproduce by causing them to metamorphose or molt prematurely.

Nontoxic sprays. Dormant-oil sprays consist of nontoxic horticultural oils derived from plants. They are applied to major trees and shrubs early in the spring during the dormant season when plants are leafless, to smother egg cases and sucking insects.

Insecticidal soaps, available commercially in spray form, work best on soft-bodied insects—aphids, mealy bugs, scales, whiteflies, spider mites, and thrips—and can be used on most garden plants including vegetable crops. Like all insecticides, they are indiscriminate and may kill beneficial insects as well. They have no residual effect and must be reapplied to catch newly arrived insects. As they may burn leaves, test insecticidal soaps by spraying on a few leaves 24 hours in advance of a general application. A satisfactory insecticidal soap can be made by mixing 3 to 6 tablespoons of a mild dish-washing soap—Ivory Liquid, Ivory Snow, Fels Naptha or other soap (not detergent)—per 1 gallon of water.

If spraying with dormant oil or insecticidal soaps does not prove sufficient over time, before resorting to more toxic chemicals, consider removing a pest-prone plant and replacing it with a more resistant variety.

Toxic Controls

Chemical pesticides are substances used to control pests and include insecticides (insects), fungicides (fungi and other pathogens) and herbicides (weeds). The safe use of all chemical pesticides hinges upon proper handling to prevent any adverse reactions upon the environment, including wildlife and aquatic organisms, which can occur through misapplication, overdose, drift and runoff. The presence of pests must be in sufficient amount to warrant the application of chemicals. Use them only as a last resort when alternative methods have failed. Identify the problem and choose the right treatment.

Diagnosing an Insect or Disease Problem

1. *Identify the plant.* Insects and diseases are specific to many plants at specific times of the year. Knowing the plant name and its common afflictions will help you to identify the pest. Positive identification is necessary as many pests cause similar symptoms on infected plants.

2. *Identify the insect.* Many bugs are clearly visible on the underside of leaves, tunneling in leaves, inside rolled-up leaves, or in cocoons or webs. Keeping garden records will alert you in advance to the approximate arrival and departure dates of insects. Although the dates may vary as the weather will effect the timing of their appearance each year, insects are predictable in their habits.

3. *Identify a bacterial or fungal disease.* Look for such symptoms as stem and root rot, wilt, putrid fruits, random dead or off-color spots in leaves, off-color or curled leaf edges, powdery mildew or scale or sudden dieback of branches. Symptoms are often more intense during wet springs, in overwatered soil and in areas with poor air circulation

4. *Applying pesticides.* Timing is crucial in the application of pesticides. Learn everything you can about the life cycles of insects as they are more vulnerable at certain developmental stages, such as larval or nymph, than others.

Read the labels carefully. Follow directions explicitly. Mix only what you need to use for the day. Spray conservatively. Do not use sprays when the temperature is over 80° or under 40° F. Spray in calm weather, either early in the morning or late in the day. Keep in mind that any spray potent enough to kill undesirable insects is likely to kill something else. Rotate your use of chemicals whenever practical. Beware of pesticides that can harm birds, animals and beneficial insects. Take great care in using any toxic materials in the vegetable garden. Systemic sprays and slug pellets are not suitable for use on edibles. To avoid killing pollinating bees, do not spray citrus or other fruit trees while in bloom.

Herbicides are used to kill weeds. Herbicide sprays will kill or damage any plant on which they fall. Systemic herbicides are absorbed by the foliage of the plant and carried internally through the vascular system of the plant to its roots. Any systemic spray falling on the soil, however, becomes inactive.

As an added precaution, wear a mask and rubber gloves when handling toxic chemicals. Launder clothing immediately after use and line-dry. Keep contaminated garments separate from other clothing. If they become saturated due to a spill of chemicals, they are best discarded.

Do not use pesticides (insecticides, miticides or fungicides) in a sprayer used for weed control. Call your local cooperative extension service for further information on controlling pest problems.

Diagnosing Symptoms of Environmental Stress

1. *Drought:* wilting on new growth in late afternoon, loss and yellowing of foliage, dieback or leaf scorch on current season's leaves. Water deeply and thoroughly (1 inch

of water a week). Amend soil to encourage water retention; mulch well. In drought conditions, thin heavily foliaged plants to cut back on transpiration.

2. *Poor drainage:* caused by faulty irrigation systems, compacted soil, construction damage or a grade change that has buried the tree's feeder roots. Discolored, wilted leaves and mildew are symptoms of either poor drainage or overwatering.

3. *Sunscald:* burning and cracking of tender, smooth bark of newly planted trees. Provide light shade or wrap trunk to protect it. Avoid reflected heat and light from buildings or paving. Choose heat-tolerant plants.

4. *Winter burn or freeze damage:* caused by sudden drops in temperature; bud, leaf and fruit drop; dieback of tender new growth; on evergreens, brown tips on previous season's growth apparent in spring. Move tender plants to shelter or provide protection.

5. *Iron deficiency (chlorosis):* leaves turn yellow starting between veins of the young growth while veins remain green; may be caused by high pH. Spray with water-soluble iron or dig iron chelates into soil.

6. *Chemical damage:* leaf discoloration, poor growth, dieback; may be caused by swimming-pool chemical. Store and mix chemicals away from planting area. Prevent pool backwash from reaching plantings. Use spray weed killers with caution to keep drift from falling on desirable plants.

7. *Salts build-up:* poor growth, loss of leaf luster; caused by runoff of highway or sidewalk salting, ocean winds. Rinse salt-sprayed plants with fresh water and irrigate heavily with fresh water in early spring to leach out winter accumulations of salts. Choose salt-tolerant varieties in beach areas and along roadways where salt is spread to melt winter ice.

Chapter 15

Scheduling Garden Chores and Recording Garden Highlights

Gardening by Season

Gardening is a year-round activity with a tempo that changes with the seasons. There is a rhythm to the year, to the times when it is necessary to undertake important tasks, to the moments when you can relax. After all, you want to enjoy your garden, admire your efforts and take in the view. Finding the rhythm of the fast and the slow periods will save you from panic and seasonal overload. One helpful system is to keep good records.

On a wall or desk-top calendar, record events in your garden—not only the planting, pruning, fertilizing and general maintenance chores that must be done every year, but also when you started seeds, the first appearance of a pest problem and its treatment. Keep a record of the weather, the temperature, the rainfall. Record successes and failures in the perennial beds, favorite cultivars, harvests of vegetables and herbs, when you planted containers and with what, the amounts of fertilizer and mulch you purchased and good local and mail-order supply sources.

Make a list of highlights in the garden as well as moments when the garden lacked interest—the day the first spring bulbs appeared, when spring-flowering trees and shrubs were in their glory, what was in bloom during the heat of summer, winter damage, the presence of resident and migrating birds and that of butterflies. Note problem areas, and design changes you intend to make, plants you want to add. In other words, draw up as complete a history of events in your garden as you can.

After a year, the sequence of those events will become apparent, and after reading this book, you should be able to identify important and secondary gardening tasks, their timing in your garden as well as ways to simplify maintenance. There are, after all, twelve months in the year during which, in many parts of the country, you at times will find yourself indoors. Even in warm climate zones, there are lulls in gardening during summer and winter months.

With a bit of study and a proper schedule, you can spread the gardening load throughout the year and avoid much of the build-up that suddenly occurs once a new growing season begins. Some tasks need to be done on time, but others can even be put off, at least temporarily.

When spring comes, you will be seeing early bulbs flowering close to the house, or along the edge of the woods, that you planted last fall. A favored broadleaf evergreen will have come through the winter undamaged because it was properly sited and kept moist during dry spells. The azaleas will be glorious because you remembered to fertilize as well as prune them last summer after they bloomed. In high summer, tender bulbs that you ordered in winter for spring planting will flower, perennials stand straight because you staked them, cool weather vegetable seedlings will be hardening off prior to being set out in the vegetable garden for fall harvest. The hillside will no longer be eroded, but covered instead with drought-resistant ornamental grasses and summer-blooming shrubs. In winter, the peeling bark of a river birch along with red-twig dogwood will grace a moist corner of the yard that was once an oasis of dull grass and weeds.

Use the following outline as a guide to tasks you may wish to record. Timing will vary depending on local weather conditions, but the sequence of events will remain the same. (Not all tasks are relevant to all gardens, and there are many others not mentioned.) Your records will become your personal calendar to managing and caring for your garden.

Winter

Time for study and planning, learning about new plants, designing new planting beds or reordering existing ones and making changes to simplify maintenance. Order seeds and plants for spring planting. In cold climates when temperatures are above freezing, begin pruning. Watch for the presence of insect problems, egg cases, evidence of borers, etc., for later treatment. Pick up storm debris, clean out woodlands and hedge rows, check winter plant protection, mulches and winter tree wrap. Clean and repair tools. In warm climates, it is time for soil preparation; major planting projects, including bare-root plants, native plants and cool-season vegetables; and starting seeds for spring and summer bloom. Set out winter annuals. Summer-flowering trees and shrubs, including roses, can be pruned. Water dry lawns.

Late Winter
In cold climates, start seeds indoors or in the cold frame. Apply dormant-oil spray for overwintering pests on ornamentals. Finish major pruning. Note trees and shrubs that need pruning after bloom. Fertilize as necessary. Service irrigation systems, mowing and spraying equipment. Check gardening supplies. In warm climates, finish pruning, fertilizing, continue planting cool-season vegetables, start planting warm-season ones. Enjoy the first spring flowers.

Spring
In the North, plant and transplant bare-root and balled-and-burlaped and container-grown trees and shrubs including fruit trees and roses, perennials, annuals and summer bulbs. Prune shrub roses and summer-flowering shrubs. Fertilize lawns, apply pre-emergent weed control. For spring cleanup, remove seasonal weeds; edge beds and borders. Dig, divide and replant overgrown summer- and fall-blooming perennials. Prepare vegetable garden and annual beds. Harden off seedlings started indoors. Begin mowing and watering if the spring is dry. Plant containers.

Early Summer
Continue planting container-grown plants. Plant tender bulbs. Prune evergreen hedges after the first flush of new growth has elongated. Prune spring-flowering shrubs after they bloom. Fertilize rhododendrons and azaleas after bloom and container plants for continuous bloom. Pinch back annuals, chrysanthemums, asters and basil to encourage bushy plants. Dig, divide and replant early spring–blooming plants. Set stakes and plant rings. Keep the garden neat, remove fallen leaves and other litter, deadhead flowers, cut back early spring–blooming plants. Destroy diseased plants promptly. Mulch to conserve moisture and discourage weeds. Begin watering, continue weeding. Harvest spring crops; replant vacant areas. Inspect plants for insects and diseases. Continue mowing.

Summer

Continue general maintenance, watering and weeding, monitoring insect and disease problems and taking appropriate action. Prune climber and rambling roses after bloom. Dig, divide and replant spring-blooming perennials after bloom. Take softwood cuttings. Harvest flowers, vegetables, herbs and fruits for immediate use or for drying. Plant fall vegetable crops. Take hardwood cuttings. As temperatures cool, seed or sod new lawns. In warm climates, start seeds for cool-season flowers and vegetables.

Early Fall

Plant major trees, shrubs and hardy spring bulbs. Prepare beds for spring planting. Record gardening successes and failures. For fall cleanup, rake and compost leaves. Continue mowing. Cut back perennials. Finish final weeding, edge beds, prepare winter plant protection and spread protective mulching. Check espaliered plants, climbing roses and vines for loose fasteners. Prepare cold frame for winter. In warm climates, begin fall planting; prepare beds for cool-season annuals and winter vegetables.

Late Fall

Water newly planted trees, shrubs, evergreens and lawns (in warm climates) before the ground freezes if the fall has been dry. Drain irrigation systems before major freeze. Apply winter mulches after the ground freezes. Clean and sharpen tools before storing. After final mowing, clean mower and drain any remaining gasoline from tank. In warm climates, begin planting spring bulbs, overseed lawns with winter rye, clean up perennial beds, dig and divide overgrown plants and plant cool-season vegetables.

Chapter 16

Garden Design for the Future

By working in our gardens, we gain an understanding of our natural environment and the planning that is necessary to organize and maintain the outdoor spaces in which we live and play and grow plants.

Our traditional approaches to garden design have come, in large part, from abroad. This, along with our choice of plants, the arrival of foreign insects and disease and our dependence on pesticides, has caused extensive environmental damage and slowed the development of a suitable American landscape style.

Foreign plants have been introduced and have run rampant (kudzu, purple loosestrife, knotweed and Hall's honeysuckle, to name a few), crowding out our native species. Pests have brought about the demise of the American chestnut to blight and the American elm to Dutch elm disease. Current threats to oaks, hemlocks and flowering dogwoods will continue to change the look of our woodlands and city streets.

We have learned the folly of monocultures and the wisdom of diversity of species. Not only do mixed plantings reduce the need for pesticides, but they withstand attacks by insects and disease that can cause the annihilation of single-species plantings. We are restoring our native prairies, bringing back and encouraging functional prairie and woodland native plants. As a nation, we are passing laws to defend the wetlands from development, thus protecting breeding grounds for many birds, fish and other water life, as well as controlling serious flooding. We are searching for solutions to chronic water shortages and to surface and groundwater contamination. We are passing laws for stricter control of the irresponsible use of pesticides and fertilizers. As landfills can no longer absorb grass clippings and other garden debris, we must learn to recycle them.

These facts suggest ways for us to approach our own gardens. If we reduce the size of areas needing mowing, curtail our use of chemical pesticides, fertilizers and herbicides, include more native and adapted plants in our planting schemes and turn our garden debris into valuable compost, we can have gardens that are functional and beautiful as well as environmentally friendly.

English-style lawns, like classic perennial borders, are the product of a cool, moist climate. Both are climatically unsuited to many parts of the United States. Costly in time as well as in the materials necessary to maintain them, ever-green, weed-free lawns and expansive borders have a tendency to affect the environment beyond the spaces for which they were intended. Lawns put heavy demands on valuable resources—water, fertilizer, herbicides and insecticides—that ultimately damage the environment, to say nothing of the time and expense of mowing. "The perfect green and weed-free" lawn can be boring in its unchanging nature.

We must base the design of our gardens on what we learn from the ecology of the land itself, its natural form, its soil, the climate surrounding it and the relationships among the native plants that grow on it. In our own gardens, we must start to protect and work with the environment, finding ways to cultivate our gardens that do not waste energy, resources and money. The topography of the land, the amount of rain that falls on it, the depth and pH range of the soil and the type of soil should be the defining factors for any design.

Within the natural environment of the site, conditions can be altered, trees planted or limbed up to create more or less shade, drainage improved, humus added to lighten the soil, water and fertilizers applied to green up the lawn and plants sprayed for pests. Over time, however, these methods bring limited success and are costly. Existing conditions may reduce our choices, but they point out the direction in which we should go, saving us, as gardeners, from struggling against self-imposed problems.

Even a small garden may contain a wet spot, a rock outcropping, a wooded corner; each of these can be enhanced to become a bog garden, a rock garden, a spring woodland garden. Meadow, prairie and chaparral gardens, desert gardens, wetland and woodland gardens, each have their unique identities formed within and highlighting the existing conditions of climate, soil, topography and plant material of their respective locales. These naturalistic gardens encourage the presence of native animals, including birds and butterflies, which add animation and beauty of their own. Native plants, and those that have successively adapted over time to a particular place and its level of rainfall, demand less water than exotic or imported plants, less fertilizer and suffer fewer pest problems.

One of the basic limitations set by our natural environment is the amount of available water. Already, we are learning to garden with less. Xeriscaping, an approach to gardening based on limited water usage, was developed in areas suffering from severe drought and year-round water shortages. Its methods can be applied to any style of landscape design and to any garden in which our aim is to conserve water and simplify maintenance.

The principles of xeriscaping are simple. They call for good planning and design, soil analysis and improvements, practical turf areas, appropriate plant selection, efficient irrigation, mulching and suitable maintenance. By converting little-used areas of lawns into beds filled with drought-tolerant trees and shrubs, by using native plants, by grouping together plants with similar water needs and by applying water efficiently, you can simplify gardening chores.

Digging planting holes 3 to 4 inches deeper than normally recommended will encourage plants to grow deeper and become more drought resistant. Conditioning soil by adding leaf mold and compost to the planting bed will increase its ability to absorb water. Spreading a 3- to 4-inch layer of mulch around plants and on unplanted soil surfaces will decrease evaporation. Plants will be healthier and therefore less prone to insects and disease than those under stress. All of these are sound gardening practices, saving you time and expense in the long-run while benefiting the plants and the garden.

Inspiration for garden design should come from within our national boundaries. Given the great diversity of climate and topography across the United States and the vast selection of available and beautiful native plants as well as the many cultural backgrounds that are represented by our citizenry, we, as gardeners, have the challenge and the opportunity to develop distinct and personal gardens that echo the surrounding American landscape and speak realistically to our ways of life.

There are many themes around which to design a garden: a historic style, interest in certain kinds of plant material, the existence of a choice tree, a view, a color scheme, a special season of the year, family life, the seaside, a special garden for the evening or the weekend. A design must consider layout, usage, form, texture, changing color, seasonal interest, maintenance requirements and the amount of time you wish to devote to your garden. Many such considerations will and should be shaped by personal preferences.

Ultimately, a garden should be a source of pleasure and interest year-round, a place of relaxation and refreshment, a changing view from the house, a drift of scent on a warm evening, the sound of splashing water—an ever-changing, involving experience.

There is no such thing as a maintenance-free garden. A garden certainly requires work, but hopefully this book has provided you with ways and means of organizing the work, of beginning and following through with knowledge, gaining experience as you go, remaining confident even when things don't come out exactly as expected.

Gardens are never static. It is their nature to grow, evolve and change. It is your reward that, along the way, they produce moments of great beauty.

Appendix

Ordering and Caring for Mail-Order Plants

When ordering seeds or plants from catalogs, make sure that the plants are hardy in the zone in which you garden, that they will tolerate your low winter temperatures, summer heat and humidity, and that your growing season is long enough for any vegetables and fruits to ripen. Most good catalogs will give you that information, but they are, after all, trying to sell plants, so if in doubt, check at your local arboretum or with your county agent. Order from a supplier who gives you the botanical name of the plant as well as its common name so you know what you are getting.

Order large container or balled-and-burlaped trees and shrubs from a grower or nursery in your zone or a colder zone. When buying a major tree or shrub, check that the soil is similar to your soil—sand, clay, loam. This helps to ensure that the plants will be acclimatized to local conditions.

Check your mail-order plants upon arrival. Open any boxes immediately as the plants need air and indirect light. Remove any packing material (plastic peanuts, wood shavings or extra paper). Place the plants upright. Live plants usually arrive in small pots. Remove any materials covering the top of the potting mixture put there to keep the soil from falling out. If the plants seem dry, give them a gentle soaking. Immerse dry pots in a bucket of tepid water until any air bubbles stop rising from the soil surface. Let them drain.

Small bare-root dormant plants may be wrapped in damp sphagnum moss or wood shavings with a tight outer wrap of clear plastic. Unwrap immediately. Their roots are probably still damp,

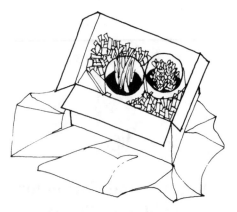

but they may have no tops and show no signs of life. Pot up in any clean potting or seed-starting soil that's available and water well. This will give the plants time to recover from being shipped and help them to grow.

If the weather is rainy or too cold when the plants arrive, they can be kept until you are ready to plant and will profit from a chance to become acclimatized. Set them aside in a sheltered corner against the house, in a garage or under trees, away from strong drying winds and in filtered or indirect light for a week to ten days.

If large bare-root plants (roses, flowering trees and shrubs) are housed in a poly-lined bag, punch holes in it, or open it up to allow the air to circulate, sprinkle the roots with water and rewrap loosely. Bare-root plants can be stored in a cool dark basement or garage for several weeks if necessary. But check roots from time to time for dryness. Sprinkle lightly if necessary. Before planting, soak roots of large plants in tepid water for up to 24 hours. Soak perennials about 30 minutes. Be patient with woody plants as they may show no signs of growth after planting until late spring or early summer. Continue watering on a weekly basis. Scratch off a small piece of bark. If the branch is green underneath, the plant is alive.

Bare-root, woody shrubs and small trees can also be potted up or heeled into the ground to protect the roots from drying out. With a spade or garden fork dig a V-shaped trench in a sheltered spot, place the roots of the woody plants in it and shove the soil back in the trench. They can be left there for several days or even weeks if the weather stays cool.

In spring you can plant mail-order plants as soon as the ground has thawed. In summer, plants can be set out in their pots or trenched out to harden in the shade as soon as you receive them, left for several days and then planted out in the sun.

Tools of the Trade

Buy the best tools you can afford for performance and durability. Keep them clean of mud and other debris. Oil them occasionally (the handles as well as the blades). Keep all cutting tools sharp. It makes work easier, faster and safer. Dull edges leave ragged, torn edges, injuring stems and roots, inviting disease and decay. When pruning, clean blades with alcohol or a 10 percent solution of clorox between cuts to avoid spreading disease if you suspect the plant may be infected.

Tools

Basics for a Small Garden

Shovel: all-purpose round-nosed garden shovel for tilling by hand, digging and moving small plants

Spade: square-nosed, for turning soil, especially clay, double digging, edging beds

Fork: for digging, dividing plants, cultivating in light soil, turning compost piles (in heavy, rocky soil a square-tined fork will stand up better than a flat-tined fork which may bend)

Rakes: a metal rake for removing small stones and dirt clods and evening up newly cultivated beds; a bamboo or plastic rake for raking leaves

Cultivator: useful for light cultivation, weeding, breaking up clods

Hand tools: trowel, transplanting trowel, hand fork, hand cultivator, asparagus knife for deeply rooted weeds, Cape Cod weeder for surface weeding, pruning clippers, shears, lopping shears, curved blade pruning saw

Watering equipment: nylon-reinforced garden hoses, soaker hoses, sprinklers, adjustable nozzle, bubbler, spray wand for hanging baskets, watering can, rain gauge

Other equipment: stakes, twine, plant labels, indelible pen, espalier nails, coated wire, gardening gloves, fungicides and insecticides, plant and weed sprayers, rubber gloves, goggles, disposable overalls, respirator if applying toxic chemicals, fertilizers, soil amenders, aged or dehydrated manure, peat moss, mulch, plastic or burlap tarp to collect garden debris, compost bin, soil-testing kit, tool caddy or gardening basket, lawn mower

Extras for a Large Garden

Wheelbarrow or *garden cart*

Irrigation system: drip irrigation system that uses emitters, mini-sprinklers that apply water to plant root zone, automatic system that uses timers

Sprayers: for insecticides and fungicides, portable sprayer with built-in pump action, or compressed-air sprayer, separate sprayer for weed control

Pole pruner
Cold frame
Shredder or *grinder* for garden wastes

Just for the Vegetable Garden

Rotary tiller: for tilling large gardens, mixing in amendments
    and fertilizers, difficult to maneuver in small spaces
    which must be finished off by hand
Hoe: for breaking up clods in newly cultivated beds, weed-
    ing, vegetable gardens
Cultivator: for loosening soil, weeding
Other equipment: stakes, poles, trellises, tomato cages, trellis
    netting, soil thermometer
Mulch: biodegradable black plastic

For Starting Seeds Indoors

Propagators or *plastic flats*
Grow lights
Plastic or *jiffy pots*
Sterile potting soil
Bottom-heat coil
Small clippers
Cultivating tools
Watering can with *rose nozzle*
Mister
Thermometer
Water-soluble fertilizer

Zone Map

The United States Department of Agriculture (USDA) Zone Map divides the country into ten climate zones. The divisions are based on the average first and last frost dates in each zone. These dates determine the length of the growing season, or frost-free days, in each zone. The zones are numbered from north to south, one through eleven; the lower the number, the colder the winter and the shorter the growing season.

Plants are assigned a hardiness rating, meaning they can survive a given low temperature reading. For instance, if a plant is said to be hardy in zones 6 through 9, it may survive the winter in zone 5 if protected, but it will succumb in zone 4. Within each zone, temperatures may fluctuate as much as 10 degrees because of variations in exposure, from the top of the hill to the bottom, the difference of north- or south-facing slopes or the proximity of a large body of water. Within your garden you may have microclimates, or pockets that intensify or moderate local conditions, that will effect hardiness.

Use the zone map as a guideline when choosing plants. Cold hardiness is not the single determining factor in a plant's hardiness. Many factors other than the intensity of winter cold determine whether plants survive. They include the duration of the cold temperatures, lack of snow cover, warm summers, dry autumns, soils, drainage, initial planting and continued care of the plants.

Frost dates are of primary importance in establishing timing for anyone planning a vegetable garden or for the planting of annuals as well as helping to determine scheduling of general gardening maintenance tasks.

Plant Lists

The following plant lists are intended as suggestions for beginning gardeners as all are relatively easy to acquire and to grow. Included are plants that will grow in a wide range of conditions and in more than two hardiness zones. They are listed by the role they play in the garden—large shade trees, ornamental and small shade trees, shrubs, vines and so forth. There are suggestions for difficult sites as

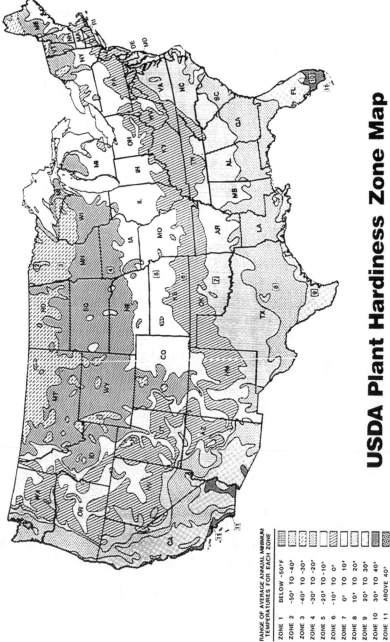

USDA Plant Hardiness Zone Map

RANGE OF AVERAGE ANNUAL MINIMUM TEMPERATURES FOR EACH ZONE		
ZONE 1	BELOW -50°F
ZONE 2	-50° TO -40°
ZONE 3	-40° TO -30°
ZONE 4	-30° TO -20°
ZONE 5	-20° TO -10°
ZONE 6	-10° TO 0°
ZONE 7	0° TO 10°
ZONE 8	10° TO 20°
ZONE 9	20° TO 30°
ZONE 10	30° TO 40°
ZONE 11	ABOVE 40°

well as plants that attract birds and butterflies. Some research will be
necessary to determine if a plant is hardy in your temperature zone
and compatible with your soil type and the moisture content of your
soil. Some, such as the maples, oaks, hollies, rhododendrons, azaleas,
viburnums, junipers and some perennials offer a broad spectrum of
species and cultivars with differing growth habits, foliage and blossom colors from which to choose.

Trees

LARGE SHADE TREES

Red maple (*Acer rubrum*)
Sugar maple (*Acer saccharum*)
Red horse chestnut (*Aesculus* x *carnea*)
River birch (*Betula nigra*)
Shagbark hickory (*Carya ovata*)

Common hackberry (*Celtis occidentalis*)
White ash (*Fraxinus americana*)
Green ash (*Fraxinus pennsylvanica*)
Honey locust (*Gleditsia triacanthos* var. *inermis*)
Kentucky coffee tree (*Gymnocladus dioicus*)
Tulip tree (*Liriodendron tulipifera*)
American sweet gum (*Liquidambar styraciflua*)
Tupelo, black gum, sour gum (*Nyssa sylvatica*)
Chinese pistachio (*Pistacia chinensis*)
London plane (*Plantanus* x *acerifolia*)
Eastern cottonwood (*Populus deltoides*)
White oak (*Quercus alba*)
Shingle oak (*Quercus imbricaria*)
Willow oak (*Quercus phellos*)
Red oak (*Quercus rubra*)
Shumard oak (*Quercus shumardii*)
Live oak (*Quercus virginiana*)
Japanese tree lilac (*Syringa reticulata*)
Japanese pagoda tree, scholar tree (*Sophora japonica*)
Little-leaf linden (*Tilia cordata*)

Silver linden (*Tilia tomentosa*)
Lacebark elm (*Ulmus parvifolia*)
Japanese zelkova (*Zelkova serrata*)

ORNAMENTAL AND SMALL SHADE TREES

Trident maple (*Acer buergerianum*)
Amur maple (*Acer ginnala*)
Paperbark maple (*Acer griseum*)
Japanese maple (*Acer palmatum*)
Shadbush, serviceberry, Juneberry (*Amelanchier arborea*)
American hornbeam, ironwood (*Carpinus caroliniana*)
Redbud (*Cercis canadensis*)
White fringe tree (*Chionanthus virginicus*)
Flowering dogwood (*Cornus florida*)
Kousa dogwood (*Cornus kousa*)
Green hawthorn (*Crataegus viridis*)
American holly (*Ilex opaca*)
Goldenrain tree (*Koelreutreria paniculata*)
Southern magnolia (*Magnolia grandiflora*)
Saucer magnolia (*Magnolia x soulangiana*)
Sweet bay magnolia (*Magnolia virginiana*)
Japanese flowering crabapple (*Malus floribunda*)
Tea crab (*Malus hupehensis*)
Sargent crabapple (*Malus sargentii*)
Malus hybrids: 'Callaway', 'Centurion', 'Donald Wyman', 'Red Jade'
Sourwood (*Oxydendrum arboreum*)
Japanese flowering cherry (*Prunus serrulata*)
Higan cherry (*Prunus subhirtella*)
Yoshino cherry (*Prunus x yedoensis*)
Bradford callery pear (*Pyrus calleryana* 'Bradford')
Japanese styrax (*Styrax japonicus*)

Shrubs

BROADLEAF EVERGREEN SHRUBS

Some of the following plants may be semi-evergreen in colder climates.

Abelia
Japanese aucuba (*Aucuba japonica*)
Azalea
Barberry (*Berberis*)
Boxwood (*Buxus*)
Camellia
Cotoneaster
Euonymus
Chinese holly (*Ilex cornuta*)
Japanese holly (*Ilex crenata*)
Inkberry (*Ilex glabra*)
Blue holly (*Ilex* x *meserveae*)
Yaupon holly (*Ilex vomitoria*)
Mountain laurel (*Kalmia latifolia*)
Leucothoe
Privet (*Ligustrum*)
Mahonia
Nandina, heavenly bamboo (*Nandina domestica*)
Japanese pieris (*Pieris japonica*)
Cherry laurel (*Prunus laurocerasus*)
Photinia
Pyracantha
Rhododendron
Skimmia
Viburnum

NEEDLE EVERGREEN SHRUBS

Juniper
Microbiota
Yew (*Taxus*)

DECIDUOUS SHRUBS

The following list of deciduous flowering shrubs includes those with more than one season of interest: outstanding foliage, colorful fruit, fall color, seed heads, bark, winter silhouette.

Butterfly bush *(Buddleia)*
Bluebeard, Blue spirea *(Caryopteris x clandonensis)*
Carolina allspice *(Calycanthus floridus)*
Sweetpepper bush, clethra *(Clethra alnifolia)*
Tartarian dogwood *(Cornus alba)*
Red osier dogwood *(Cornus sericea)*
Dwarf fothergilla *(Fothergilla gardenii)*
Hydrangea
Virginia sweetspire *(Itea virginicus)*
Winter jasmine *(Jasmine nudiflorum)*
Crape myrtle *(Langerstroemia indica)*
Japanese kerria *(Kerria japonica)*
Star magnolia *(Magnolia stellata)*
Bumald spirea *(Spiraea x bumalda)*
Viburnum

Trees and Shrubs for Difficult Sites

Moist sites: red oak *(Acer rubrum)*, river birch *(Betula nigra)*, franklinia *(Franklinia alatamaha)*, American sweet gum *(Liquidambar styraciflua)*, sweet bay magnolia *(Magnolia virginiana)*, Virginia sweetspire *(Itea virginica)*, holly *(Ilex* spp.), Eastern cottonwood *(Populus deltoides)*, willow *(Salix* spp.), arborvitae *(Thuja occidentalis)*.

Dry or alkaline sites: Turkish hazelnut *(Corulus colurna)*, Russian olive *(Elaeagnus angustifolia)*, Chinese pistacia *(Pistacia chinensis)*, green ash *(Fraxinus pennsylvanica)*, goldenrain tree *(Koelreuteria paniculata)*, bur oak *(Quercus macrocarpa)*, pine *(Pinus* spp.), juniper *(Juniperus* spp.), Japanese scholar tree *(Sophora japonica)*.

Trees and shrubs for naturalized sites: shadbush, serviceberry, Juneberry *(Amelanchier arborea)*, river birch *(Betula nigra)*, shagbark hickory *(Carya ovata)*, redbud *(Cercis canadensis)*, tulip tree *(Liriodendron tulipifera)*, sweet bay magnolia *(Magnolia virginiana)*, tupelo *(Nyssa sylvatica)*, sourwood *(Oxydendron arboreum)*, sassafras *(Sassafras albidum)*.

Vines

Kiwi vine *(Actinida)*
Akebia
Trumpet vine *(Campsis radicans)*
Clematis
Carolina jessamine *(Gelsemium sempervirens)*
Ivy *(Hedera helix)*
Climbing hydrangea *(Hydrangea anomala petiolaris)*
Honeysuckle *(Lonicera sempervirens)*
Virginia creeper *(Parthenocissus quinquefolia)*
Boston ivy *(Parthenocissus tricuspidata)*
Silver-lace vine *(Polygonum aubertii)*
Wisteria

Ground Covers

European ginger *(Asarum europeum)*
Epimedium
Heaths and Heather *(Calluna* and *Erica)*
Wintercreeper *(Euonymus fortunei radicans)*
Hosta
Hardy ice plant *(Delosperma cooperi)*
Sweet woodruff *(Galium odoratum)*
Ivy *(Hedera)*
Daylily *(Hemerocallis)*
Aaronsbeard St. Johnswort *(Hypericum calcynum)*
Dead nettle *(Lamium maculatum)*
Lily turf *(Liriope muscari)*
Pachysandra *(Pachysandra terminalis)*
Sedum
Lamb's ear *(Stachys byzantina)*
Periwinkle *(Vinca minor)*

Many low, spreading shrubs can also be used for ground covers:

Nikko slender deutzia *(Deutzia gracillis)*
Winter jasmine
Juniper
Cotoneaster
Low azaleas
Roses (some)

Perennials

The following perennials are valuable for long lasting foliage and good growth habit as well as bloom.

Lady's mantle *(Alchemilla mollis)*
Artemisia
Astilbe
Baptisia *(Baptisia australis)*
Hardy begonia *(Begonia grandis)*
Bergenia
Pinks, carnations *(Dianthus)*
Cranesbill *(Geranium)*
Christmas and Lenten rose *(Hellebore)*
Daylily *(Hemerocallis)*
Coralbell *(Heuchera)*
Hosta
Candytuft *(Iberis sempervirens)*
Siberian iris *(Iris siberica)*
Hardy ferns
Ornamental grasses
Peony
Pulmonaria
Sedum
Lamb's ear *(Stachys byzantina)*
Yucca

Annuals

Hardy Annuals: ageratum, sweet alyssum, begonia, catharanthus, celosia, cleome, coleus, geranium *(Pelargonium)*, gompherina, impatiens, lobelia, marigold, mimulus, morning glory, nasturtium, nicotiana, petunia, poppy, snapdragon, zinnia.

Annuals for cutting: baby's breath *(Gypsophila elegans)*, bells-of-Ireland, bishop's flower *(Amni majus)*, calendula, China pink *(Dianthus chinensis)*, cosmos *(Cosmos bipinatus)*, feverfew *(Chrysanthemum parthenium)* larkspur, snapdragon, pansy, salvia *(Salviaf arinacea)*, scabiosa or pincushion flower, statice, stock, sweet pea, zinnia.

Annuals and Perennials with Fragrant Flowers or Foliage

Achillea
Artemisia
Giant hyssop *(Agastache)*
Sweet alyssum
Daylily *(Hemerocallis)*
Four-o'clock *(Mirabilis jalapa)*
Scented geranium
Hosta
Lavender
Lily *(Lilium* spp.)—Royal Lily, Aurelian hybrids
Mignonette *(Resada odorata)*
Monarda
Nasturtium
Nicotiana sylvestris
Peony
Petunia
Pink carnation
Garden phlox *(Phlox paniculata)*
Sage
Stock *(Matthiola longipetala, M. incana)*
Sweet pea
Sweet rocket *(Hesperis matrionalis)*
Sweet sultan *(Centaurea moschata)*

Sweet woodruff *(Galium odoratum)*
Wallflower *(Cheiranthus cheii)*

Plants That Attract Butterflies

Annuals and perennials: black-eyed Susan, butterfly milkweed *(Asclepias tuberosa),* cosmos, gaillardia, gayfeather *(Liatris),* goldenrod, globe amaranth, heliotrope, impatiens, ironweed *(Veronia),* joe-pye weed, lantana, lupine, marigold, monarda, mignonette, pentas, phlox, purple coneflower, scabiosa, sunflower, sweet william, tithonia, verbena and zinnia.

Shrubs and vines: butterfly bush *(Buddleia davidii),* Dropmore scarlet honeysuckle, Dutchman's-pipe vine.

Plants That Attract Birds

Trees, shrubs and vines: American holly, hackberry, hawthorn, cherry, plum, Eastern red cedar, magnolia, mulberry, flowering dogwood, Sargent crabapple, tulip poplar, sassafras, mountain ash, serviceberry, American cranberry, viburnum, elderberry, firethorn, Tartarian honeysuckle, currant, gooseberry, blueberry, huckleberry, *Rosa rugosa, Rosa wichuriana,* bayberry, buckeye, coralberry, albizia, Siberian pea shrub, fragrant sumac, creeping cotoneaster, juniper, bearberry, crowberry, bunchberry, sweetfern, grapes, Hall's honeysuckle, trumpet vine and Virginia creeper.

Hummingbirds are attracted to tubular-shaped blossoms. Primarily nectar eaters, they prefer red and orange flowers. Among favorites are scarlet runner bean, morning glory, nasturtium, hollyhock, tithonia, scarlet sage, snapdragon, four-o'clock, zinnia, phlox, columbine, petunia, fuchsia, delphinium, larkspur, impatiens, *Salvia officianalis,* nicotiana, cleome, foxglove and sweet william.

Many "weeds" or native wildflowers attract butterflies and birds: butterfly weed, milkweed, clover, nettles, thistles, black-eyed Susan, coneflowers, clover, sunflowers, ragweed, amaranth, lamb's-quarters, sheep sorrel, bristle grass and panic grass.

Vegetable Planting Calendar
Sow seeds unless indicated to set out plants*

ZONE-FROST DATE

NAME	ZONE 4 LAST: JUNE 10 FIRST: AUG. 20	ZONE 5 LAST: MAY 20 FIRST: SEPT. 20	ZONE 6 LAST: APR. 20 FIRST: OCT. 10	ZONE 7 LAST: MAR. 20 FIRST: OCT. 30	ZONE 8 LAST: FEB. 20 FIRST: NOV. 20	ZONE 9 LAST: JAN. 30 FIRST: DEC. 20
ARTICHOKE, globe	May 15	May 15–June 10	Apr. 10–May 1	Mar. 20–Apr. 1	Feb. 5–Apr. 1	unsuitable
ASPARAGUS (plants)	May 15–June 1	Apr. 20–May 15	Mar. 15–Apr. 15 Mar. 15–July 1	Feb. 1–Mar. 10 Nov. 15–Dec. 31	unsuitable Jan. 15–Mar. 15	unsuitable Jan. 1–Feb. 1
BEANS, broad	Apr. 15–July 15	Apr. 1–June 1	Aug. 1–Sept. 1	Feb. 15–Mar. 15 Aug. 1–Sept. 1	Sept. 1	Oct. 1–Dec. 1
BEANS, lima	unsuitable	unsuitable	May 1–June 20	Apr. 1–Aug. 1	Mar. 1–Sept. 1	Feb. 1–Oct. 1
BEANS, scarlet runner	June 1–Aug. 15	May 15–Aug. 1	Apr. 15–Aug. 1	Mar. 15 Aug. 1	Feb. 1 Aug. 1	Feb. 1 Oct. 1–Dec. 1
BEANS, snap	unsuitable	May 15–July 1	Apr. 25–July 20	Mar. 15–Aug. 15	Mar. 1–May 1 July 1–Sept. 10	Feb. 1–Apr. 1 Sept. 1–Nov. 1

*See Zone Map on page 125

	ZONE 4	ZONE 5	ZONE 6	ZONE 7	ZONE 8	ZONE 9
BEETS	May 15–June 15	Apr. 25–July 1	Mar. 20–July 25 Aug. 1–Sept. 1	Feb. 15–May 15 Sept.1–Dec. 1	Jan. 20–Apr. 1 Sept. 1–Dec. 31	Jan. 1–Mar. 15
BROCCOLI (plants)	May 1–June 10	May 1–June 15	Mar. 25–Apr. 20 June 15–July 15	Feb. 15–Mar. 15 July 1–Aug. 15	Jan. 15–Feb. 15 Aug. 1–Sept. 15	Jan. 1– Jan. 30 Sept. 1–Dec. 31
BRUSSELS SPROUTS (plants)	May 1–June 10	May 1–June 15	Mar. 25–Apr. 20 June 15–July 15	Feb. 15–Mar. 15 July 1–Aug. 15	Jan. 15–Feb. 15 Aug. 1–Sept. 15	Jan. 1–Jan. 30 Sept. 1–Dec. 31
CABBAGE (plants)	May 20–June 1	May 1–June 15	Mar. 10–Apr. 1 June 1–July 15	Feb. 1–Mar. 1 Aug. 1–Sept. 1	Jan. 1–Feb. 25 Sept. 1–Dec. 1	Jan. 1–Jan. 15 Sept. 1–Dec. 1
CANTALOUPE	unsuitable	June 1–July 1	May–June 1	Apr. 1–May 30	Mar. 15–May 15	Feb. 20–Apr. 1
CARROTS	May 15–June 15	May 1–July 1	Apr. 1–July 20	Feb. 15–Mar. 20 July 1–Aug. 15	Jan. 15–Mar. 1 Sept. 1–Nov. 1	Jan. 1–Mar. 1 Sept. 15–Dec. 1
CAULIFLOWER (plants)	May 1–June 15	May 1–July 1	Mar. 15–Apr. 20 June 1–July 25	Feb. 10–Mar. 10 July 15–Aug. 15	Jan. 10– Feb. 10 Aug. 1–Sept. 15	Jan. 1–Feb. 1 Sept. 15–Nov. 1
CELERY and CELERIAC (plants)	June 1–June 15	May 10–July 1	May 10–July 15	Apr. 1–Aug. 15	Jan. 20–Feb. 10 July 15–Sept. 1	Jan. 1–Feb. 1 Oct. 1–Dec. 1
CHAYOTE	Feb. 10–Mar. 1	Mar. 5–Apr. 15	Apr. 1–May 1	May 1	unsuitable	unsuitable
CHERVIL	May 10–June 10	Apr. 15–June 15	Mar. 10–Apr. 10	Feb. 10–Mar. 10	Jan. 1–Feb. 1 Nov. 1–Dec. 31	Jan. 1–Feb. 1 Nov. 1–Dec. 31

❧ 135

	ZONE 4	ZONE 5	ZONE 6	ZONE 7	ZONE 8	ZONE 9
CHINESE CABBAGE	May 15–June 15	May 1–July 1	June 15–Aug. 1	Aug. 1–Sept. 1	Sept. 15–Oct. 15	Sept. 1–Dec. 1
CHIVES	May 10–June 10	Apr. 15–June 15	Mar. 10–Apr. 10	Feb. 10–Mar. 10	Jan. 1–Feb. 1 Nov. 1–Dec. 31	Jan. 1–Feb. 1 Nov. 1–Dec. 31
COLLARDS (plants)	May 20–June 15	May 1–June 15	Mar. 10–Aug. 1	Feb. 15–May 1 Aug. 1–Sept. 15	Jan. 1–Mar. 15 Aug. 25–Nov. 1	Jan. 1–Feb. 15 Sept. 1–Dec. 31
CORN	unsuitable	May 15–July 1	Apr. 25–July 10	Mar. 15–Aug. 1	Feb. 20–Apr. 15 June 1–Sept. 1	Feb. 1–Mar. 15
CORN SALAD (MACHE)	May 15–June 15	Apr. 15–Aug. 1	Feb. 15–Apr. 15 Aug. 15–Sept. 15	Jan. 1–Mar. 15 Sept. 15–Nov. 1	Jan. 1–Mar. 15 Oct. 1–Dec. 31	Jan. 1–Feb. 15 Oct. 1–Dec. 31
CUCUMBERS	unsuitable	June 1–June 15	May 1–July 1	Apr. 1–Aug. 1	Feb. 15–Apr. 15 June 1–Aug. 15	Feb. 1–Mar. 15 Aug. 15–Oct. 1
EGGPLANT (plants)	unsuitable	June 1–June 15	May 10–June 15	Apr. 1–July 1	Feb. 20–Aug. 1	Feb. 1–Mar. 1 Aug. 1–Sept. 30
ENDIVE	May 15–July 1	May 1–July 15	Mar. 25–Apr. 15 July 1–Aug. 15	Mar. 1–Apr. 1 July 15–Aug. 15	Jan. 15–Mar. 1 Sept. 1–Oct. 1	Jan. 1–Mar. 1 Sept. 1–Dec. 31
GARLIC	May 15–June 1	Apr. 15–May 15	Mar. 10–Apr. 1	Feb. 1–Mar. 1	Aug. 15–Oct. 1	Sept. 15–Nov. 15
GOURDS	unsuitable	June 1	May 1–May 15	Apr. 1–May 1	Mar. 1–Apr. 1	Feb. 20–Apr. 1 Aug. 1–Sept. 1

	ZONE 4	ZONE 5	ZONE 6	ZONE 7	ZONE 8	ZONE 9
JERUSALEM ARTICHOKE	June 5	May 20	May 1–May 15	Apr. 1–May 1	Mar. 15–Apr. 15	Feb. 15 June 1–Dec. 1
JICAMA	Feb. 20	Mar. 15	Apr. 15	May 1	unsuitable	unsuitable
KALE	May 15–June 15	Apr. 20–July 1	Mar. 20–Apr. 10 July 1–Aug. 1	Feb. 20–Mar. 10 July 15–Sept. 1	Jan. 20–Feb. 10 Aug. 15–Oct. 15	Jan. 1–Feb. 1 Sept. 1–Dec. 31
KOHLRABI	May 15–June 15	Apr. 20–July 15	Mar. 20–May 1 July 1–Aug. 1	Feb. 20–Mar. 10 Aug. 1–Sept. 1	Jan. 20–Feb. 10 Sept. 1–Oct. 15	Jan. 1–Feb. 1 Sept. 1–Dec. 31
LEEKS	May–June 1	May 1–July 15	Mar. 15–Apr. 15	Feb. 1–Mar. 1	Jan. 1–Feb. 15 Sept. 1–Nov. 1	Jan. 1–Feb. 1 Sept. 15–Nov. 1
LETTUCE, leaf	May 15–July 15	May 1–Aug. 1	Mar. 20–May 15 July 15–Sept. 1	Feb. 1–Apr. 1 Aug. 15–Oct. 1	Jan. 1–Mar. 15 Sept. 1–Nov. 1	Jan. 1–Feb. 1 Sept. 15–Dec. 31
MELON	unsuitable	May 1–June 15	May 1–June 15	Apr. 1–July 15	Feb. 15–Apr. 15	Feb. 15–Mar. 15
MUSTARD	May 15–July 15	May 1–Aug. 1	Mar. 20–Aug. 15	Feb. 20–Apr. 1 Aug. 15–Oct. 15	Feb. 15–Apr. 15 Sept. 1–Dec. 1	Jan. 1–Mar. 1 Sept. 15–Dec. 31
OKRA	unsuitable	June 1–June 20	May 1–July 15	Apr. 1–Aug. 10	Mar. 1–Sept. 10	Feb. 1–Oct. 1
ONION (plants)	May 1–June 10	Apr. 20–May 15	Mar. 15–Apr. 10	Feb. 10–Mar. 10	Jan. 1–Jan. 15 Oct. 1–Dec. 31	Jan. 1–Jan. 15 Oct. 1–Dec. 31

	ZONE 4	ZONE 5	ZONE 6	ZONE 7	ZONE 8	ZONE 9
ONION (seeds)	May 1–June 10	Apr. 20–May 15	Mar. 15–Apr. 1	Feb. 10–Mar. 10	Jan. 1–Jan. 15 Sept. 1–Nov. 1	Jan. 1–Jan. 15 Sept. 15–Nov. 1
ONION (sets)	May 1–June 10	Apr. 20–May 15	Mar. 10–Apr. 1	Feb. 1–Mar. 20	Jan. 1–Jan. 15 Nov. 1–Dec. 31	Jan. 1–Jan. 15 Nov. 1–Dec. 31
PARSLEY	May 15–June 15	May 1–July 1	Mar. 20–Aug. 1	Feb. 15–Mar. 15 Aug. 1–Sept. 15	Jan. 1–Jan. 30 Sept. 1–Dec. 31	Jan. 1–Jan. 30 Sept. 1–Dec. 31
PARSNIPS	May 15–June 10	May 1–June 15	Mar. 20–June 1	Feb. 15–Mar. 15 Aug. 1–Sept. 1	Jan. 1–Feb. 1	Sept. 1–Dec. 1
PEAS, black-eyed	unsuitable	unsuitable	May 10–July 1	Apr. 1–Aug. 1	Mar. 1–Sept. 1	Feb. 15–May 1 July 1–Sept. 20
PEAS, garden	May 10–June 15	Apr. 15–July 15 Aug. 1–Aug. 15	Mar. 10–Apr. 10 Aug. 1–Sept. 15	Feb. 1–Mar. 15 Oct. 1–Dec. 1	Jan. 1–Mar. 1 Oct. 1–Dec. 31	Jan. 1–Feb. 15
PEAS, podded	May 10–June 15	Apr. 15–July 15 Aug. 1–Aug. 15	Mar. 10–Apr. 10 Aug. 1–Sept. 15	Feb. 1–Mar. 15 Oct. 1–Dec. 1	Jan. 1–Mar. 1 Oct. 1–Dec. 31	Jan. 1–Feb. 15
PEPPERS (plants)	unsuitable	May 25–June 20	May 10–June 1	Apr. 10–July 20	Mar. 1–Aug. 15	Feb. 1–Apr. 1 Aug. 15–Oct. 1
POTATOES	May 15–June 15	Apr. 15–June 15	Mar. 15–June 15	Feb. 10–Mar. 15 July 20–Aug. 10	Jan. 15–Mar. 1 Aug. 10–Sept. 15	Jan. 1–Feb. 15 Aug. 1–Sept. 15

	ZONE 4	ZONE 5	ZONE 6	ZONE 7	ZONE 8	ZONE 9
PUMPKIN	unsuitable	May 20–June 10	June 1–July 1	June 10–July 10	July 1–Aug. 1	Aug. 1–Sept. 1
RADISHES	May 1–July 15	Apr. 15–Aug. 15	Mar. 10–May 10 July 15–Sept. 15	Jan. 20–May 1 Aug. 15–Oct. 15	Jan. 1–Apr. 1 Sept. 1–Dec. 1	Jan. 1–Apr. 1 Oct. 1–Dec. 31
RHUBARB (plants)	May 15–June 1 Sept. 1–Oct. 1	Apr. 15–May 10 Sept. 15–Nov. 1	Mar. 10–Apr. 10 Oct. 15–Nov. 15	Nov. 1–Dec. 1	unsuitable	unsuitable
RUTABAGAS	May 15–June 15	May 1–June 20	June 15–July 15	Jan. 15–Mar. 1 July 15–Aug. 1	Aug. 1–Sept. 1	Oct. 15–Nov. 15
SHALLOTS	May 10–June 1	Apr. 20–May 10	Mar. 1–Apr. 15	Feb. 1–Mar. 10	Jan. 1–Feb. 20 Aug. 15–Oct. 1	Jan. 1–Feb. 1 Sept. 15–Nov. 1
SOYBEANS	unsuitable	unsuitable	May 10–June 25	Apr. 10–July 15	Mar. 10–July 30	Mar. 1–July 30
SPINACH	May 1–July 1	Apr. 10–Aug. 1 Aug. 1–Sept. 1	Mar. 1–Apr. 15 Sept. 1–Oct. 1	Jan. 15–Mar. 15 Oct. 1–Dec. 31	Jan. 1–Mar. 1 Oct. 1–Dec. 31	Jan. 1–Feb. 15
SPINACH, Malabar	June 10	June 1–July 1 July 1–Aug. 1	Apr. 20–May 1 June 1–Aug. 15	Apr. 1–Apr. 15	Mar. 15–Apr. 15	Feb. 20–Apr. 1
SPINACH, New Zealand	unsuitable	May 20–June 15	May–July 15	Apr. 1–Aug. 1	Mar. 1–Aug. 1	Feb. 1–Apr. 1 June 1–Oct. 1
SQUASH, summer	June 10–June 20	May 15–July 1	May 1–July 15	Apr. 1–Aug. 1	Mar. 1–Aug. 1	Feb. 1–Oct. 1

	ZONE 4	ZONE 5	ZONE 6	ZONE 7	ZONE 8	ZONE 9
SQUASH, winter	unsuitable	May 20–June 10	June 1–July 1	June 10–July 10	July 1–Aug. 1	Aug. 1–Sept. 1
SWEET POTATOES	unsuitable	unsuitable	May 20–June 10	Apr. 10–June 15	Mar. 20–July 1	Feb. 15–July 1
SWISS CHARD	May 15–June 15	May 10–July 1	Apr. 1–July 20	Feb. 20–Sept. 10	Jan. 20–Apr. 15 June 1–Oct. 1	Jan. 1–Apr. 1 June 1–Dec. 31
TOMATILLO	Feb. 10–Apr. 1 Sept. 1	Mar. 1–Apr. 1	Apr. 1–May 1	May 1	May 15	June 5
TOMATOES (plants)	June 15–June 30	May 25–June 20	May 5–June 20	Apr. 1–July 1	Mar. 1–Aug. 1	Feb. 1–Apr. 1
TURNIPS	May 15–June 30	Apr. 15–July 15	Mar. 10–June 15	Feb. 10–Mar. 10 Aug. 1–Sept. 15	Jan. 10–Mar. 1 Sept. 1–Nov. 15	Jan. 1–Mar. 1 Oct. 1–Dec. 31
WATERMELON	unsuitable	June 15–July 1	May 1–June 15	Apr. 1–July 15	Feb. 15–July 30	Feb. 15–Mar. 15

Herbs for the Kitchen and Potpourri

NAME Botanical name	STATUS	HEIGHT	PROPAGATION	CULTURE	USES	COMMENTS
ANGELICA Angelica archangelica	biennial	to 7'	seed	rich, moist soil; cool, partially shady site; feed occasionally	culinary (candy)	spectacular effect in back of border or along stream edge
BASIL Ocimum basilicum	annual	18"	seed or transplant	moderately rich soil, sun, partial shade, keep watered	basic culinary herb (freeze or dry); potpourri	pinch back to thicken; 'Dark Opal' is a decorative garden addition
BAY Laurus nobilis	tender perennial	to 10'	cuttings	average, well-drained soil; protect from burning sun and wind	culinary; potpourri; topiary and dry arrangements	grow as a container plant, and bring indoors in frosty areas
BERGAMOT Monarda didyma	perennial	24" to 36"	seed or transplant	moist, fairly rich, slightly acidic soil; partial shade	culinary; potpourri	showy blossom, white through pink, red, purple and mahogany; subject to mold
BORAGE Borago officinalis	annual	24" to 36"	seed	good drainage, averge soil, sun	culinary (in summer drinks and candy)	clusters of brilliant blue flowers, attractive to bees
CALENDULA Calendula officinalis	annual	12" to 24"	seed	rich, loamy soil; full sun	culinary (in salads; petals dried as substitute for saffron)	showy blossoms from yellow to orange, single and double; edible addition to salads

	STATUS	HEIGHT	PROPAGATION	CULTURE	USES	COMMENTS
CATMINT *Nepeta cataria*	perennial	24" to 36"	seed or division	well-drained, moist, alkaline soil; sunny to semishade	potpourri	attracts bees; beautiful blue flowers
CHERVIL *Anthriscus cerefolium*	annual	12" to 18"	sow directly	moderately rich soil, keep moist	culinary (in salads and soup, egg, fish and chicken dishes; use fresh)	very hardy; plant in early spring; make repeated sowings for continuous supply
CHIVES *Allium schoenoprasum*	perennial	12" to 18"	seed or division	rich soil, high in phosphorus; sun to partial shade	classic kitchen herb; freeze chopped leaves	rosy purple blossom is decorative in the garden as well as edible; will self-seed
CORIANDER *Coriandrum sativum*	annual	12" to 36"	seed	light, well-drained soil; full sun; keep moist	culinary (leaves and seeds useful for flavor and scent; dry seeds for cooking or potpourri,basic herb in Indian, Chinese and Mexican dishes)	also called Chinese parsley or cilantro
DILL *Anethum graveolens*	annual	24" to 36"	seed	average, well-drained soil; protect from strong win; staking may be necessary	culinary (use seeds and leaves, fresh or dried)	best planted in clumps against wind damage; for continuous supply, remove flowers to prevent going to seed